THE BREXIT REFERENDUM ON TWITTER

THE BREXIT REFERENDUM ON TWITTER

A Mixed-Method, Computational Analysis

JINGRONG TONG
The University of Sheffield, UK
LANDONG ZUO
Independent Researcher, UK

emerald PUBLISHING

United Kingdom – North America – Japan
India – Malaysia – China

Emerald Publishing Limited
Howard House, Wagon Lane, Bingley BD16 1WA, UK

First edition 2021

British Library Cataloguing in Publication Data
A catalogue record for this book is available from the British Library

ISBN: 978-1-80043-295-6 (Print)
ISBN: 978-1-80043-294-9 (Online)
ISBN: 978-1-80043-296-3 (Epub)

Printed and bound by CPI Group (UK) Ltd, Croydon, CR0 4YY

CONTENTS

LIST OF FIGURES

LIST OF TABLES

To Daniel

ABOUT THE AUTHORS

Jingrong Tong is Senior Lecturer in Digital News Cultures at the University of Sheffield. Her research focuses on the impact of digital technology on journalism, social media analysis and environmental communication.

Landong Zuo is an IT consultant and data scientist specialised in data mining, data analysis and Nature Language Processing. His research interests include data integration, analysis and visualisation in the fields of Semantic Web, Linked Data and Big Data.

ACKNOWLEDGEMENTS

Some content of the book, in particular, that in Chapter 3, is developed (reprinted) from our research article: "Mainstreaming populism through the Twitter practices of politicians and the news media: A case study of the 2016 Brexit referendum debates," published by *Information Polity* in 2020. The publication is available at IOS Press through DOI: 10.3233/IP-190197. The authors would like to thank IOS Press for granting us the right to include the related content in this book. The authors want to thank the two anonymous reviewers for their comments. Thanks also go to the open-source applications including Twitter4J, Elasticsearch, Kibana, Gephi and Inskape, their contributors and Python communities online. The authors would like to thank Jen McCall of Emerald Publishing for her enthusiasm and support for this book project, which is our second book about Brexit and Twitter. The first one is *Tweeting the Environment #Brexit*, published in 2018 by Emerald.

1

INTRODUCTION

As part of an academic effort to understand social media communication, this book offers an insight into how Twitter works in shaping political discourse through a case study of the United Kingdom's (UK's) European Union (EU) referendum in 2016. On 23 June 2016, the UK voted to leave the EU by 52–48%. With the departure of the UK from the EU on 31 January 2020, its 47 years of EU membership ended, hopefully along with the four-year post-Brexit vote chaos, shaping the geopolitical order of the European region and of the world. Scholars have tried to figure out what happened at the time of the Brexit vote. Given the growing popularity of social media among populations and its increasing significance in the public communication sphere, one of the questions scholars want to answer is about the role played by social media in the referendum. Particularly, what, and how, was the political discourse about the referendum formed on social media?

To answer this question, the research reported in this book examines three aspects of Twitter communication about the referendum: (1) social representations of the referendum, (2) the tweeting practices of key British politicians and news media, and (3) ordinary users' responses to David Cameron (@David_Cameron), the Prime Minister at the time of the referendum, and Nigel Farage (@Nigel_Farage), the then leader of the UK Independence Party (UKIP). This study contributes to the existing literature about social media communication as well as Brexit studies (see, for example, Agarwal, Singh, & Toshniwal., 2018; Grčar, Cherepnalkoski, Mozetič, & Novak, 2017).

In this study, the mixed-method, computational analysis of over 12 million of tweets reveals a dual role played by Twitter in the referendum: (1) clarifying and contrasting public opinion between Leave and Remain supporters; and (2) legitimising, mainstreaming and spreading the ideology of populism. The research identifies the importance of the tweeting practices of users – including

British politicians, the news media and ordinary users – in shaping the political discourse about the referendum. This study reveals that, as a result of their tweeting practices, divided opinion was explicitly expressed on Twitter, mirroring divergent collective understandings of the UK's EU membership and suggesting the existence of ideological confrontation between Leave and Remain supporters in Twitter communication. Twitter showed its capacity to facilitate political manipulation and spread the ideology of populism through articulating and mainstreaming populist claims into the political debate about the referendum. The social media strategies of populist politicians and Brexit supporters demonstrated their well-developed understanding of how Twitter works in shaping political discourse, which, however, appeared to have been misunderstood by the Remain camp. The influence of populist politicians, who fluently, tactically and actively used the social site to promulgate their populist ideas, was amplified.

This Introduction chapter will explore the critical issues related to the Brexit referendum and the social dynamics behind the referendum outcome in the first part and then review the existing studies on social media and Brexit. Afterwards, it will introduce the methodology of this research, such as data collection, the pipeline of data analysis and research methods and procedures. It will conclude with a reflection on the limitations of this study.

THE BREXIT REFERENDUM, EURO-SCEPTICISM AND POPULISM

The Brexit vote confirms the existence of a profound divide in public opinion between Remain and Leave supporters– this divide was palpable ahead of the referendum (Bonikowski, 2017; Freeden, 2017; Gusterson, 2017; Habermas, 2016).[1] While the Remain vote was in favour of European integration and globalisation, right-wing Euro-sceptic populism and English nationalism were underlying the Leave vote (Corbett, 2016). The sharp polarisation in the vote was coherent with the context of gradually increasing Euro-scepticism and populism.

Before the referendum, Britain saw a surging tide of Euro-scepticism, referring to scepticism towards the benefits of European integration and the UK's EU membership (Boomgaarden, Schuck, Elenbaas, & Vreese, 2011; Eichenberg & Dalton, 1993). Euro-scepticism started to get stronger from the

1 https://whatukthinks.org/eu/ (Accessed on June 12, 2018).

mid-1980s when the press and social actors began to stress British 'differentness' (Spiering, 2004, p. 127). Especially in the past decade, domestic and international factors deepened the British population's scepticism towards the EU. Some of the most prominent factors were the UK's social and economic inequalities, the crisis in the National Health Service (NHS), the global financial crisis, the Euro-zone crisis, the exodus of refugees fleeing from the war zones in the Middle East and Africa to Europe since 2014 and an increase in the number of terror attacks in the West. In 2015, more than a quarter of Britons viewed that 'European unification has already gone too far', with only some 28% of respondents thinking positively about British 'unification should be pushed further' (Vasilopoulou, 2016, p. 219). Against this backdrop, in the 2015 UK General Election, David Cameron promised to hold a referendum on the UK's EU membership.

As suggested by the polls, before the Brexit referendum, public opinion was divided between Remain and Leave.[2] The Leave and Remain camps – mainly comprising politicians, political campaigns, the news media, banks, companies and other elite members such as economists and entrepreneurs – advocated their own arguments and foci. The Leave camp pushed to establish a new relationship between the UK and the EU, while the Remain camp promoted maintaining the current connection. The primary concerns of the former were immigration (freedom of movement) and the financial costs of the UK's EU membership. The arguments of the latter focused on the economy (free market), the global leadership of the UK and national security that the UK could gain by staying within the EU (Vasilopoulou, 2016). In particular, the theme of immigration was the Leave camp's 'powerful campaign frame' (Vasilopoulou, 2016, p. 222; Hobolt, 2016). The economy – the worry over the economic ramifications of the Brexit vote – was the real emphasis of the Remain camp (Hobolt, 2016).

Before the referendum, the division between Leave and Remain cut across political parties. Such a division existed within (rather than between) mainstream political parties and among party leaders and members of parliament (MPs). While the Conservative Party declared to stay neutral, David Cameron and George Osborne sided with Remain, and Brexiteer politicians, such as Boris Johnson and Michael Gove, supported Leave. Within the Labour Party that pledged to support Remain, Jeremy Corbyn, adopting a Remain stance, clashed with Euro-sceptic Labour MPs who led the (unofficial) Labour Leave campaign. The Green Party and the Liberal Democrats were split between Remain and Leave.

2 https://whatukthinks.org/eu/ (Accessed on June 12, 2018).

Likewise, before the referendum, news media outlets officially declared their support for Remain or Leave (Hobolt, 2016). With *The Sun*, The *Daily Telegraph*, The *Sunday Times* and the *Daily Mail* supporting Leave, The *Guardian*, the *Independent*, The *Times*, the *Financial Times* and the *Daily Mirror* were in favour of Remain (Loughborough University, 2016). These divisions reflect that the nation was divided by ideologies and demographics – in particular, 'the divide between winners and losers of globalisation' (Hobolt, 2016, p. 1259).

The arguments of the Leave camp mirror the values of nationalist populism, which has surged in Western democratic societies, such as the UK, the US, France and Italy. While acknowledging there are different perspectives of, and contextual variations in, the concept of populism, this book uses the term as an anti-establishment ideology that juxtaposes the interests of 'the people' against those of the 'elites' and 'others' (Bonikowski, 2017; Engesser, Ernst, Esser, & Büchel., 2017; Gusterson, 2017; Inglehart & Norris, 2016). The critical elements of the populist ideology include 'emphasising the sovereignty of the people', 'advocating for the people', 'attacking the elites', 'ostracising others' and 'invoking the heartland' (Engesser et al., 2017). However, populism can also be a type of 'discursive strategy selectively employed by political outsiders' to try to change the political status quo (Bonikowski, 2016).

In the UK, populism was marginal compared to the (once-)dominant ideologies of globalisation and European integration. For many years, the majority of the British population favoured EU membership. In the 1975 UK European Communities (EC) membership referendum, more than two-thirds of voters voted to continue EC membership.[3] Recently, however, populism rose amid the emergence of Euro-scepticism and the anti-globalisation movement (Taggart, 2004). As discussed above, global issues, such as the EU migration crisis, fuelled the rise of populism.

The surge of populism in the UK and Europe was evident in the recent electoral successes of populist political parties, such as the UKIP and the French National Front. In Italy, for example, in 2018, voters supported populist parties – the Five Star Movement and the League – to lead the next government. In the wake of these electoral victories of populist parties, populism has increasingly entered mainstream politics and become a mainstream political discourse (Akkerman, Lange, & Rooduijn, 2016; Curran, 2004; Mondon, 2013). Such populism presents the features of nationalist populism, expressing hostility towards immigrants (Gusterson, 2017) and

3 The European Communities (EC) were 'fushioned' into the European Union from 1993 (Von Bogdandy & Nettesheim, 1996).

stressing the sovereignty of the nation-state. It defends the interests of those who have been economically disadvantaged under the influence of globalisation and neoliberalism. Such populism is seen by Bonikowski as a conflation of nationalism and populism (2017).

The arguments of nationalist populism were embodied in those of the Leave camp, who stressed the necessity to protect national interests and the interests of locals. They opposed the dominant neo-liberal political values that embrace globalisation and internationalism. Fervently, right-wing political actors, such as Nigel Farage and Boris Johnson, called to 'take back control' and curb immigration. Their strident advocacy was ardently supported by right-wing news outlets like *The Sun* and The *Daily Telegraph*. However, the publicity of particular political values like populist claims in news coverage is still subject to the gate-keeping of news practitioners.

SOCIAL MEDIA AND THE BREXIT REFERENDUM

The traditional news media used to be one of the primary platforms for political communication, where public opinion and interests were represented, and where the public was informed. Proliferating rapidly, social media sites, such as Twitter, have shown an increasing importance in the political communication landscape, providing alternative platforms for channelling or reflecting public opinion (Anstead & O'Loughlin, 2015; Sobkowicz, Kaschesky, & Bouchard, 2012). Users use the technological affordances of social media to gather, to express their views, and to be heard on these social sites (Gerbaudo, 2018b).

Most of the existing studies examining Twitter communication explore the capacity of Twitter to motivate and enable participation in politics. Different aspects of Twitter communication have been studied, such as interactions and network structures (Al-garadi, Varathan, & Ravana, 2016; Colleoni, Rozza, & Arvidsson, 2014; Gunnarsson Lorentzen, 2014; Himelboim, Hansen, & Bowser, 2013; Horan, 2013; Lindgren & Cocq, 2017; Meraz & Papacharissi, 2013), political sentiments (Baviera, Peris, & Cano-Orón, 2019; Ceron, Curini, Iacus, & Porro, 2014; Dang-Xuan, Stieglitz, Wladarsch, & Neuberger, 2013), topics and discourses (Evans & Evans, 2016; Evolvi, 2019; Horan, 2013; Pond & Lewis, 2019), the use of Twitter (Bode & Dalrymple, 2016b; Bruns & Highfield, 2013; Coesemans & Cock, 2017; Ellison & Hardey, 2013; Enli & Skogerbø, 2013; Graham, Broersma, Hazelhoff, & Haar, 2013; Graham, Jackson, & Broersma, 2016; Klinger, 2013; Lachlan & Levy, 2016; Larsson &

Ihlen, 2015; Larsson & Moe, 2014), and the impact of Twitter (Baviera et al., 2019; Karlsen & Enjolras, 2016). Some of these studies have recognised the potential of Twitter to reflect public opinion among users and to enhance political participation (Graham et al., 2016; Ifukor, 2010; Meraz & Papacharissi, 2013).

In their efforts to understand the role played by social media in the Brexit referendum, scholars have examined the Twitter use, campaign strategies and opinions of Leave and Remain groups (see, for example, Fanoulis & Guerra, 2017; Gorodnichenko, Pham, & Talavera, 2018; Llewellyn & Cram., 2016; Usherwood & Wright, 2017). Not surprisingly, they have found the polarisation between the Leave and Remain users in social media communication about the Brexit referendum (see, for example, Del Vicario, Zollo, Caldarelli, Scala, & Quattrociocchi, 2017; Hall, Tinati, & Jennings, 2018). They have also identified the correlation between users' political interests and their social media participation during the event (Bossetta, Segesten, & Trenz, 2018). Social media sites have been thought to play a crucial role in facilitating the rise of nationalist populism and in misleading the British electorate (Sunstein, 2018). Scholars (see, for example, Lopez, Cesar, Collignon-Delma, Benoit, & Matsuo, 2017) even regard that analysing public opinion expressed on Twitter can predict the Brexit vote. Joining other research exploring public opinion on social media (see, for example, Anstead & O'Loughlin, 2015; Elmer, 2013; Franch, 2013; Sobkowicz et al., 2012; Bogen, Millman, Huntington, & Orchowski, 2018; Hong & Kim, 2016; Öztürk & Ayvaz, 2018), these studies about the Brexit referendum and social media can advance our understanding of what public opinion was formed on social media about the referendum.

However, the existing studies on social media and the Brexit referendum have not discussed how social media worked in shaping public opinion on their sites during this event. In particular, if the public opinion expressed on Twitter was polarised and populism was spread on social media as argued by the scholars cited above, how did this polarisation and the spread of populism happen on social sites? Answering this question can offer an insight into the role played by social media in shaping the political discourse about the referendum, in particular, and, in general, political communication in the social media era. To fulfil this aim, the research reported in this book examined three aspects of Twitter communication about the referendum: (1) how and what public understanding of the EU membership was conveyed in Twitter communication about the referendum; (2) whether, and how, the tweeting practices of key politicians and news media helped to mainstream populism; and (3) how ordinary users responded to David Cameron and Nigel Farage on Twitter.

METHODOLOGY NOTES

With a focus on Twitter communication, the research adopted mixed methods, including computational thematic analysis, topic modelling, social network analysis and traditional content analysis involving manual coding of the tweets. Methodologically, the book offers an example of, and a reflection on, how to combine mixed methods – not only quantitative and qualitative methods but also human (manual) coding and computational methods – in social media research.

Twitter, a social media platform, has been successful in attracting users since its launch in 2016. It had 15.8 millions of users in the UK in 2016 and 0.2 billion daily active users in the first quarter of 2020 (The Economist, 2020).[4] In addition to its popularity, Twitter has become one of the primary venues through which information is produced, consumed and disseminated (Brena et al., 2019). Therefore, it is pertinent to the topic under discussion in this study.

We collected and archived 12,644,199 relevant tweets published in the English language in real time one month before (including) 23 June 2016 (the date of the referendum) by using the Twitter streaming Application Programming Interface (API).[5,6] Twitter allows and provides 'companies, developers, and users with programmatic access to Twitter data' through their APIs. It defines Twitter data as reflecting 'information that users choose to share publicly', and their 'API platform provides broad access to public Twitter data that users have chosen to share with the world'.[7]

We only collected the tweets that were publicly accessible and contained any of the seven hashtags: '#Referendum', '#VoteLeave', '#VoteIn', '#EUref', '#VoteOut', '#VoteStay' and '#Brexit'. Hashtags suggest the meaning of tweets (Zappavigna, 2015). The use of these hashtags indicates users' intention to link their tweets to the topic of the referendum. The trend over time of tweets (Fig. 1.1) shows that the tweeting activity of users significantly increased when approaching the referendum day. Although these tweets collected were

4 Accessed on December 6, 2018, at https://www.statista.com/statistics/271350/twitter-users-in-the-united-kingdom-uk/.

5 We have analysed and discussed part of the data set in other publications such as Tong & Zuo, 2018 and Tong & Zuo, 2017.

6 The API is a common way of collecting Twitter data. See the documentation and discussion of the Twitter API, at https://developer.twitter.com/en/docs/tweets/timelines/FAQ (Accessed on July 7, 2020).

7 https://help.twitter.com/en/rules-and-policies/twitter-api (Accessed on July 7, 2020).

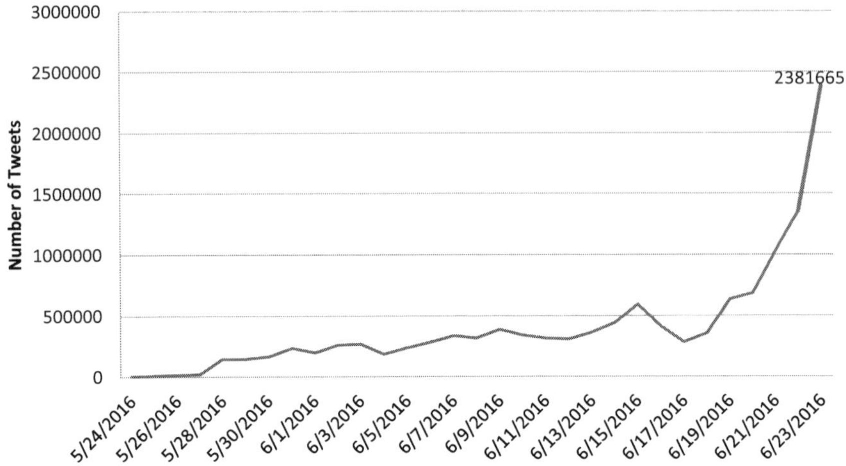

Fig. 1.1. Trend Over Time of Referendum Tweets One Month Leading to the Referendum Day.

publicly accessible, in order to protect users, we have anonymised users and their tweets if they are not public figures.

The choice of the hashtags used for data collection was made based on our two-step observation of the use of hashtags on Twitter conducted at the start of data collection. We first collected and analysed a small sample of tweets to obtain an initial understanding of the use of hashtags by users. Meanwhile, we also read related tweets in real time to understand how hashtags were used on Twitter. Informed by the observation of how Twitter users used hashtags, we decided which hashtags were the most relevant and thus should be used to collect data. Judgement and decision-making are necessary for social science research. Judgement is 'central to understanding human action' and social science research inevitably involves judgement in research process such as design and analysis (Huberty, 2000; Flyvbjerg, 2001, p. 4).

We combined computational and qualitative methods in our analysis and took on a 'hybrid' and 'computational approach to qualitative analysis' of our large-scale data (Evans, 2014; Lewis, Zamith, & Hermida, 2013). We used computational analysis to capture the overall patterns in the data and to identify small-scale (but most relevant) data from the whole dataset for detailed analysis next steps. Besides, the results of the computational study of tweets were also used to support the qualitative analysis of the identified small-scale data. After analysing the trend over time of the tweets collected and having an initial exploration of the data, we used different methods and procedures to investigate the three aspects of Twitter communication. Fig. 1.2 shows the

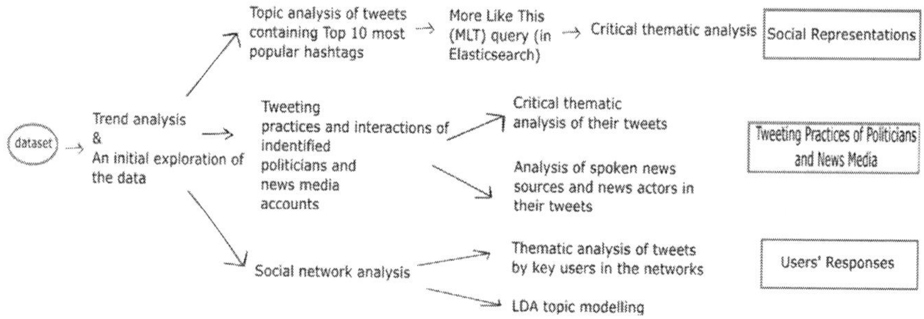

Fig. 1.2. Mapping the Overall Data Analysis Pipeline.

overall pipeline of data analysis in the whole process. The results obtained from all steps of the investigation contributed to developing our arguments and conclusion about the research topic.

Aspect 1: Social Representations of the Referendum

To examine the social representations aspect of Twitter communication, we conducted a four-phase analysis starting with an exploration of the tweeting practices of users to get an overview of the data. We, for example, examined the top 10 most popular users and hashtags. Judged by their popularity and the percentages of the tweets containing them, the top 10 hashtags were deemed as the most popular hashtags. The tweets containing any of the top 10 hashtags accounted for some 88.5% of all 12,644,199 tweets. The literal meanings of the top 10 hashtags suggest attitudes – Leave, Remain or Neutral – towards the referendum (Table 1.1).

As we wanted to focus on the tweets suggesting attitudes towards the referendum, we used the top 10 most popular hashtags as an indicator. We included tweets containing any of the top 10 hashtags that suggest Leave or Remain (8,685,749 altogether, accounting for some 68.7% of all pre-referendum tweets) for the key (meaningful) word analysis in the second phase. Meaningful words refer to content words and some phrases, such as 'vote_leave', which have actual meanings. Aiming to understand the main topics in these tweets, we analysed the significant terms of these tweets by using Elasticsearch and Kibana.[8,9] In Elasticsearch, 'unusualness' is used to measure the significance of a word: 'a term is

8 See 'What is Elasticsearch' at https://www.elastic.co/what-is/elasticsearch (Accessed on July 7, 2020).

9 See 'What is Kibana used for' at https://www.elastic.co/what-is/kibana (Accessed on July 7, 2020).

Table 1.1. The Top 10 Most Popular Hashtags in the Pre-referendum Tweets.

Hashtags	Occurrences	Attitudes
#brexit	5,515,540	Leave
#euref	3,940,985	Neutral
#voteleave	3,706,489	Leave
#remain	589,774	Remain
#eu	505,722	Neutral
#voteremain	446,264	Remain
#strongerin	395,622	Remain
#leaveeu	328,366	Leave
#inorout	288,181	Neutral
#takecontrol	274,680	Leave

considered significant if there is a noticeable difference in the frequency in which a term appears in the subset and in the background'.[10] In this research, our subset was the 8,685,749 tweets containing any of the top 10 hashtags suggesting Leave or Remain before (including) the referendum day. The, background' referred to all pre-referendum tweets in the dataset. For the present study, we ran the chi-squared test to identify the key words. We considered the p values ($p \leq 0.0000000$), chi-square scores and frequencies of significant terms, removed miscellaneous words, such as 'implement' and 'fascinating', but included the key (meaningful) words that we regarded as the most significant for categorisation. We then categorised them according to the topics indicated by the key words (Table 1.2). In the process, we also examined tweets containing any of these key words to help our categorisation.

In the third phase, we used the Elasticsearch function 'More Like This (MLT) query' to look for tweets containing any of the key (meaningful) words in the Leave and Remain categories (in Table 1.2) published in the month leading to the referendum.[11] This function also allowed us to rank the tweets according to their relevance scores. Relevance scores of the tweets – the scores derived from term frequency and inverse document frequency (TF-IDF) of the

10 https://www.elastic.co/guide/en/elasticsearch/reference/current/search-aggregations-bucket-significantterms-aggregation.html (Accessed on October 4, 2018).

11 https://www.elastic.co/guide/en/elasticsearch/reference/2.4/query-dsl-mlt-query.html (Accessed on July 7, 2020).

Table 1.2. The Topics Suggested by the Key (Meaningful) Words ($p \leq 0.0000000$).

Topics	Indicating Words
Leave	voteleave, vote_leave, leaveeu, takecontrol, control, freedom, free, leaveeuofficial, stop, projecthope, betteroffout, voteout, outside, independenceday, vote_leavemedia, takebackcontrol, lexit, labourleave, fight4uk, scaremongering, ivotedleave, projectfear, euistheproblem, scare, stop_the_eu, fishingforleave, euvoteleave23rd, strongerout, beleave, ukleave_eu, leavethe_eu, controlling
Remain	remain, strongerin, voteremain, stay, votein, Bremain, labourin, labourinforbritain, intogether, strongerinpress
Referendum (neutral)	choice, option, inorout, backing, supports, vote, campaign, eureferendum, voting, poll, polls, ivoted, debate, campaigning, undecided, postal, eudebate
EU or related issues/countries	EU, Turkey, Brussels, flag, membership, burn, reform, materials, rule, Dutch, protestor, Eurozone, reformed, Serbia, Macedonia
The news media	bbcdebate, itveuref, bbcqt, marr, itv, c4debate, audience, mailonline
Immigration	immigration, immigrants, borders, migration, uncontrolled, migrant, Calais
The economy	thrive, Labour, money, trade, jobs, pay, workers, spend, Dyson, fishermen, wages, fishing, taxes, bankers, economists, pensions, millionaire, manufacturers, prosper, CBI, JCB, spends, tariffs, scam
Laws and regulations	law, laws, regulation
Democracy	democracy, lying, unaccountable, undemocratic, dodgy, dictatorship
Muslim/Islam	Muslim, Muslims, Islamic, Ramadan
Other topics about Britain	Britain, sovereignty, army, NHS, safer, security, patriotic_brit, rights, save, better, fairer, brighter

tweets – were measured respectively against selected key (meaningful) words in each category.[12] The tweets having higher relevance scores were ranked higher

12 https://www.elastic.co/guide/en/elasticsearch/guide/current/scoring-theory.html (Accessed on July 7, 2020).

on the final list of selection output. We assessed the final selection list to remove less relevant tweets, such as those conveying no actual meaning, and then selected the top 4,000 tweets for each category, which were regarded as the most relevant in each category, for further qualitative analysis.

In the final phase of the analysis of the social representations aspect, we did a critical thematic analysis of the content of the 8,000 tweets with an emphasis on analysing the use of anchoring and objectification (Höijer, 2010). A critical thematic analysis examines not merely what themes are 'recurring, repeating and forceful' and in which ways but also the reasons for their recurrence, repetition and forcefulness by taking into account the influence of broader social ideologies and values (Antony & Thomas, 2010; Lawless & Chen, 2019). 'Anchoring' includes 'naming, thematisation, antinomies and metaphors'. 'Objectification' refers to 'ontologisation' or 'personification'. 'Ontologisation' means the attachment of something concrete to something abstract, while 'personification' concerns the human qualities attributed to non-living things. The analysis was guided by a series of analytical questions, such as: What was associated with the EU membership? How was it named? What themes were developed concerning the membership? Which metaphors were used? Any oppositions or antinomies were made? Besides, we looked for different types of anchoring, such as 'thematic anchoring' and 'emotional anchoring' (Höijer, 2011). The former means anchoring at the thematic level that embodies categories of concepts or meanings, while the latter refers to establishing the explicit link between objects and familiar emotions such as fear, hope and sympathy.

Furthermore, in this stage, after having identified the main themes in the critical thematic analysis, we also explored them in the whole database. For example, when a strong theme of the 'dictatorship' of the EU emerged in the qualitative analysis, we then examined the patterns and content of relevant data in the dataset, i.e. the tweets containing the word 'dictatorship' or 'dictator'. Although 'dictatorship' may trigger fear, this counts as 'thematic anchoring' because of the lack of a direct link between this word and the emotion of fear.

Aspect 2: Tweeting Practices of Key British Politicians and News Media

The analysis of the tweeting practices of key British politicians and news media was conducted in two steps. We identified key media and politician Twitter accounts as the first step. We included nine British politicians, who were important members of their political parties and held different attitudes towards the referendum (Table 1.3). All of them were among the top 1,000 most popular users. We excluded @michaelgove, because, in our dataset, this account did not send any original relevant tweets before the referendum. We also included 13 Twitter accounts of 12 British news outlets (Table 1.4), which also appeared among the top 1,000 most popular users. In the case of The *Times*, given The *Sunday Times* and *Times* had different stances towards the referendum, this study included both papers' Twitter accounts. We then analysed the tweeting practices of, and interactions between, these two groups, the activity level of their accounts and the popularity of their tweets. The level of activity was measured by the number of original tweets sent by a Twitter account. The level of popularity was determined by the number of tweets – including the number of original tweets published by an account and that of retweets its tweets had received in the dataset.

On the second stage, we conducted a critical thematic analysis (discussed earlier in this chapter) of the content of the original tweets published by the Twitter accounts of these politicians and news media outlets. In our analysis, after importing all the tweets onto NVivo, we repeatedly read and explored them, looking for frequently occurring words and phrases. Then, we qualitatively coded the tweets and analysed the codes in search of the main issues, agendas and arguments in their tweets. We finally examined what ideologies and values were embodied in these words, phrases and themes. Apart from the critical thematic analysis, we paid attention to the communicative strategies and styles of politicians' tweets. For the tweets of the news media, we also coded and categorised spoken news sources – whose words were quoted – in media tweets, to identify whose views were given publicity by the news media

Table 1.3. Twitter Handles of Nine Key British Politicians and Their Political Affiliations and Attitudes towards the Referendum.

Names	Political Parties	Attitudes	Twitter Handles
Boris Johnson	Conservative	Leave	@BorisJohnson
Caroline Lucas	Green	Remain	@CarolineLucas
David Cameron	Conservative	Remain	@David_Cameron
George Osborne	Conservative	Remain	@George_Osborne
Jeremy Corbyn	Labour	Remain	@jeremycorbyn
Nick Clegg	Liberal Democrats (LibDem)	Remain	@nick_clegg
Nicola Sturgeon	Scottish National Party (SNP)	Remain	@NicolaSturgeon
Nigel Farage	UKIP	Leave	@Nigel_Farage
Sadiq Khan	Labour	Remain	@SadiqKhan

Table 1.4. Thirteen Twitter Handles of Key British News Media and Their Attitudes towards the Referendum.

News Media	Attitudes	Twitter Handles
BBC	Unclear	@BBCNews
Channel 4	Unclear	@Channel4News
ITV	Unclear	@itvnews
Sky	Unclear	@SkyNews
Daily Express	Leave	@Daily_Express
Daily Mail	Leave	@DailyMailUK
Daily Mirror	Remain	@DailyMirror
Guardian	Remain	@guardian
Independent	Remain	@Independent
Daily Telegraph	Leave	@Telegraph
Sun	Leave	@TheSun
Sunday Times	Leave	@thesundaytimes
Times	Remain	@thetimes

in their tweets. For politicians who were identified as spoken news sources in the analysis, we also coded their stances towards the referendum. Besides, we analysed the frequency of the appearance of key politicians as news actors who were mentioned in the news media tweets.

Aspect 3: Users' Responses to Politicians

In the three-step analysis of users' responses to politicians in this part of the research, we chose to focus on examining their responses to David Cameron (@David_Cameron) and Nigel Farage (@Nigel_Farage). As key figures in the Remain and Leave camps, both politicians were active and very popular during the sampling time. @Nigel_Farage sent out 155 tweets, which were retweeted for 31,326 times. The 178 tweets published by @David_Cameron received 9,105 retweets.

We first used Gephi, an open-source software, to analyse the social networks surrounding @David_Cameron and @Nigel_Farage.[13] In this step, we wanted to understand who retweeted the tweets of the two politicians the most

13 https://gephi.org/.

and what attitudes they had towards the referendum and the two politicians. 'Retweeting' is an important response of users to the tweets published by the politicians. After a series of repeated tests, we chose to focus on core networks, which are networks between users with out-degree≥30.[14] Core networks are the backbones of the networks surrounding the two politicians. In other terms, this research sees these users who retweeted any of the two politicians more than 30 times as key users in the networks surrounding the two politicians.

In the second step, in order to understand their attitudes towards the referendum and the two politicians, we qualitatively analysed the themes of the tweets published by the key users in the core networks identified in the first step. In our thematic analysis, we followed the six-phase analysis process proposed by Braun and Clarke (Braun & Clarke, 2006). The tweets were coded with a focus on the users' attitudes towards and their comments on the politicians and the referendum. Other features of their tweeting activities, such as the use of hashtags, were also taken into consideration when determining their referendum stances and attitudes to the two politicians. The social network analysis and thematic analysis of the tweets of these users contributed to our understanding of the nature of the networks surrounding the Twitter handles of David Cameron and Nigel Farage and the attitudes towards the two politicians held by Twitter users who extensively retweeted or mentioned them.

In the third step, we did topic modelling of all tweets, mentioning either @David_Cameron (107,710 tweets) or @Nigel_Farage (119,318 tweets), contained in the whole dataset. In so doing, we wanted to understand the related users' attitudes to the two politicians. We applied 'latent Dirichlet allocation (LDA) topic modelling' in Python, using the Python Natural Language Toolkit and Gensim library (Blei, Ng, & Jordan, 2003; Rehurek & Sojka, 2010). LDA is

> *...a popular probabilistic topic modelling algorithm that, for each of a pre-determined and optimal number of topics, outputs a set of words accompanied by values that represent the probability of each word to be associated with the given topic*
>
> *(Bonacchi, Altaweel, & Krzyzanska, 2018, p. 178).*

After considering the coherence scores and repeating tests, we estimated that the optimal number of topics was seven. With an attempt to get an in-depth

14 The value of out-degree is the amount of times/frequencies of users' retweeting of the messages sent by the Twitter account under examination.

knowledge of relevant tweets, we then qualitatively explored the tweets containing the prominent keywords indicating topics, such as 'dodgy' and 'pencilgate'.

REFLECTIONS ON THE LIMITATIONS OF THE RESEARCH

The research reported in this book has benefited from the combination of computational and qualitative analysis of the tweets and tweeting practices of users. In particular, it treasures the advantages of using computational analysis to detect overall patterns and topics as well as to scale down large-scale data for qualitative analysis. On the one hand, given the scale of the data, it would be hard and time-consuming to analyse the whole dataset without using computational tools like Elasticsearch, Kibana and Gephi and methods like 'MLT query', social network analysis and LDA topic modelling. The findings emerging from the computational analysis not only enriched our understanding of the data but also informed the design of qualitative research. On the other hand, it was essential to conduct qualitative research to achieve a thorough understanding of the patterns in the data revealed by the computational analysis. The combination of computational and qualitative research enabled us to explore the overall picture presented in the data and, at the same time, to interpret the meanings of that picture.

However, we acknowledge that this mixed-method study may be limited by the way the research was designed, including data collection and analysis, and the judgements made in the process. For instance, our data may be influenced by our sampling strategy and the choice of hashtags in data collection. We would not claim that the dataset used for analysis in this study contains or resembles all Twitter data on the referendum in the run-up to the event. In addition, limited by the sampling time, the findings present a relatively static and short-term – instead of longitudinal – picture of Twitter communication on this topic. When it comes to data analysis, with the assistance of computational methods, we selected data for a detailed and qualitative examination – rather than focusing on statistically representative data of the whole dataset. The findings thus may be limited by the computer-assisted selections and decisions made by the researchers in the process, such as the choice of hashtags in data analysis, the selection of key (meaningful) words and topics in topic categorisation, as well as the inclusion of particular tweets but exclusion of others for thematic analysis and for the analysis of spoken news sources and news actors.

What is evident from this research is that the use of social media platforms like Twitter is going to play an increasingly important role in electoral and political debates and that political parties and politicians will seek to maximise their use of the medium. In future research, researchers may want to examine the longitudinal expression of political opinion on social media as well as the long-term tweeting practice of users. It would be helpful to examine the activity of a broader range of actors, a wider range of social media platforms and the impact of the social media practices of politicians on the news media. Additionally, useful insights can be gained from comparing the content of the traditional news media with their content published on social media. In the analysis, it would also be helpful to incorporate data obtained from other sources and by using other methods such as interviews with politicians and related users, voter turnouts, censuses, polling and political campaigning. In so doing, a more contextualised, in-depth understanding of social media practices and their interactions with offline dynamics can be achieved.

THE STRUCTURE OF THE BOOK

Apart from this introduction chapter, this book contains three chapters addressing each of the three aspects of Twitter communication and a conclusion chapter. Chapter 2 examines how the attitudes towards the EU referendum were conveyed on Twitter before the referendum, using the framework of social representations theory – in particular, the concepts of 'anchoring' and 'objectification'. The analysis reveals the expression of different – and even polarised – public understanding of the UK's EU membership. One understanding defended the established social system in which the UK was closely tied with the EU through its membership. Therefore, it saw the EU membership as necessary and beneficial to the UK. The other, however, portrayed the EU to be a failure and a barrier to the development of the UK. It, thus, proposed to break down the status quo by leaving the EU. Such expressions were made by connecting the EU membership with everyday objects.

Chapter 3 examines how the tweeting practices of British politicians and the news media contributed to mainstreaming populism in the debate about the Brexit referendum on Twitter. The communicative freedom of politicians and the extensive attention given to them by users enabled populist arguments to be presented as a legitimate part of the debate about the referendum.

Meanwhile, the news media paid overwhelming attention to politicians with a focus on the issues of immigration and the economy in their tweets. The sphere of legitimate controversy was thus created, where populist arguments appeared in parallel with those supporting globalisation and European integration. In this case, the Twitter practices of British politicians and news media led to the extensive – but largely uncritical – presence and articulation of populist claims on Twitter. Their strong presence, alongside pro-EU and pro-globalisation arguments, gave these populist perspectives a central place in the debate about the referendum. The mainstreaming of populism through the Twitter practices of politicians and the news media is inextricably linked with (and thus needs to be understood within) the broader context of rising populism where the (once-)dominant ideologies of globalisation and European integration are in decline.

In Chapter 4, we explored how Twitter users responded to David Cameron (@David_Cameron) and Nigel Farage (@Nigel_Farage) before the referendum. Social media research has found that social media users would choose to expose to information that supports, rather than challenging, their views, and they would like to interact with those who share their values. Such practice may result in the formation of political 'echo chambers' or homophily on social media. The analysis in this study, however, reveals the importance of political disagreement. In this case, political polarisation was profound, and political disagreement led to an ideological confrontation in the responses of users, particularly Leave users. Hailing @Nigel_Farage as a hero, Leave users put @David_Cameron under siege and denounced him as a 'liar'. On Twitter, they actively declared their Leave stance, legitimised Nigel Farage, but delegitimised David Cameron. They extensively retweeted and mentioned @David_Cameron in their tweets because they disagreed with him. The strategic Twitter practices of Leave users raise a question about the role played by the social media platform in the referendum.

The conclusion chapter evaluates the role of Twitter in the referendum debates in particular and in political communication in general. It is argued that Twitter, facilitating the expression of polarised public sentiments and the spread of populism, does not show great promise for serving democracy. Twitter communication, as demonstrated in this case, can be used to stir up populist sentiments, which are likely to be seen as a menace to the health of British politics and democracy – despite populism may also be thought of as a correction to politics. Populist politicians, supported by Leave users, actively and strategically used the social site of Twitter to promulgate their populist ideas. By contrast, despite actively using Twitter, the Remain campaign appeared to have misunderstood the way in which Twitter works in shaping political discourse. In this sense, the hope of social media being able to serve democracy is low. It is down to individual users to understand how social media works and how to use them for the good of democracy and politics. Meanwhile, in addition to the need to reinvigorate the news media, appropriate regulatory interventions in the social media communication space will help enhance the potential contribution of social media communication to democracy.

2

SOCIAL REPRESENTATIONS OF THE EU REFERENDUM ON TWITTER

Drawing on social representations theory, this chapter discusses what, and how, social representations of the UK's EU membership were constructed on Twitter one month before the 2016 UK-EU referendum through the processes of anchoring and objectification. Social representations refer to knowledge and understanding of things that are collectively shared and communicated among the members of a social group (Moscovici, 2001; Moscovici & Markova, 1998). Anchoring and objectification are two common processes in producing social representations. 'To anchor is... to classify and to name something', while objectification turns something abstract into something concrete and in everyday life (Moscovici, 2001, p. 49). In our study, the analysis of social representations of the membership was aimed to explore not only what but also how social representations were produced on Twitter. In particular, we analysed how the UK's EU membership was associated with familiar concepts like democracy and objectified into everyday objects, such as the NHS and immigration, in tweets, and what social representations of the EU membership were created in these processes. In so doing, we sought to understand what, and how, the meanings of the EU membership were generated through being linked with familiar concepts and everyday objects on Twitter, which is an important aspect of how Twitter works in shaping political discourse.

The study shows a clear – though relatively static – screenshot of what happened in the realm of public opinion on Twitter in the month leading up to the referendum. The analysis reveals the articulation of two contrasting understandings of the UK's EU membership. One understanding advocated continuing the established relationship between the UK and the EU because the EU membership was advantageous to the UK. The other, however, depicted the EU as a disaster, a sinking boat, and the origin of problems faced by Britain. It argued that the EU membership would only drag the UK into the abyss of crisis and thus the UK should withdraw from the EU. These two types of public understanding were expressed through associating the membership with everyday objects and familiar concepts. This case provides us with implications for understanding the importance of concrete everyday objects and familiar concepts in producing and articulating the meanings of abstract political objects in everyday (tweeting) practices.

TWEETING AS AN EVERYDAY PRACTICE

As discussed in the Introduction social media communication is often interpreted and examined as political participation (Bekafigo & McBride, 2013; Bode & Dalrymple, 2016a; Park, 2013). Scholars have studied the strategies and efforts of social media users to convey political messages during political events or protests, as exemplified in the refugee crisis (Pilipets & Winter, 2017) and the Gezi uprising in Turkey (Arda, 2015).

However, in this book, we examined social media used as an everyday practice. With the ubiquitous use of social media in everyday lives, social media communication has become an everyday practice (Manovich, 2009). Most of the studies exploring social media communication as everyday practices focus on audiences or users' use of social media for personal purposes, like leisure, entertainment, education or relationship maintenance (see, for example, Cox, 2013; Gonzalez-Polledo, 2016; Trottier, 2012). For instance, examining users' experiences of sharing visual materials, Schreiber argued that visual communication on social media is part of 'everyday communicative practices', embedded in everyday life contexts (Schreiber, 2017).

Some studies have found that political messages can be conveyed, and political meanings can be created through everyday life practices. For example, the 'everyday leisure and entertainment practices' of Kenyans were thought to have facilitated the 'development and civic engagement' in Kenya (Tully & Ekdale, 2014). In the current literature, however, few studies have examined how everyday objects and familiar concepts are used by social media users to create meanings of political objects and ideas (Lugg, 2013; Tantawi & Rosson, 2019; Zappavigna & Zhao, 2020). This topic is, nevertheless, important. It can advance our knowledge of how users make sense of and express their understanding of abstract political ideas, such as that of the EU membership, through associating them with everyday objects and familiar concepts in everyday social media practices.

SOCIAL REPRESENTATIONS THEORY

Moscovici's social representations theory regards that collective understandings and cognitions of particular objects are agreed by and shared among the members of a social group as common knowledge (Moscovici, 2001; Moscovici & Markova, 1998). Common knowledge is formed in history and in events that are collectively experienced by community members in society. It gives particular objects meanings so that individuals can easily understand them. The gaining of knowledge about objects enables individuals to establish an orderly system of values to facilitate making life decisions in the fast-changing world. Creating social representations is 'to make something unfamiliar, or unfamiliarity itself, familiar' (Moscovici, 2001, p. 37). The whole process goes through two stages of 'anchoring' and 'objectification' (Moscovici, 2001). The term 'anchoring' refers to a symbolic means of integrating the unfamiliar into familiar objects, categories or settings, the meanings of which are socio-culturally shared among a group of people. The stage of 'anchoring' involves naming and attributing features to objects. It produces a framework of interpretation. 'Objectification' refers to a process where abstract concepts or objects become concrete through being associated with those concrete (but often limited or selected) ones.

Social representations are not merely about public understanding of objects but also about communicating about it in public communication (Moscovici, 2001; Uphama, Lis, Rieschc, & Stankiewiczd, 2015). The news media was one of the primary platforms of public communication on which the population was informed and updated about understandings and meanings of objects. A considerable number of studies have examined the relationship between the news media and social representations of objects (see, for example, Uphama et al., 2015). Despite naturalising 'social thinking' and generating 'collective cognition' (Höijer, 2011, p. 3), media representations of objects, shaped by organisational factors and journalistic values, such as the political stance of news media outlets and their pursuit of maximum profits, are not identical to the social representations of these objects.

Social media offers opportunities for researchers to examine social representations of objects. Such opportunities, however, may be restricted by factors, such as the uncertainty of who users are, users' access to social media and their willingness to express views. In this study, for example, in theory, Leave and Remain supporters could 'equally' benefit from social media to 'freely' promote their respective values, circumventing the gate-keeping function of the news media. However, in practice, their social media practices might have been influenced by factors, such as their personal motives, interests, skills or understandings of how social media sites work to form public opinion.

Most of the studies on social media and social representations examined social representations of objects in relation to science, health, technology and the environment (see, for example, Kang, Ha, & Velasco, 2017; Veltri, 2013; Veltri & Atanasova, 2017). Despite its importance, social representations of political objects on social media have received little research attention.

Underlying social representations of political objects are political values about these objects held by the members of a social group. Political values are values or value orientations toward political objects (Almond & Verba, 1963). In a society, dominant political values offer the basis for policymaking, outline objectives, and set up strategies for achieving these objectives. Ruling governments and political elites often articulate dominant political values during the process of making policies and decisions about what a country should or should not do. Dissenting political values, of course, may emerge opposing the dominant ones and criticising the established social order. Other members of elites or the general public may initiate such opposition. The emergence of dissenting political values can lead to shifts of power or social change with the potential to shape the destiny of a country. Elections or referenda are the events where the general public, whose values may differ from dominant political values, can join the decision-making process. An analysis of social representations of political objects on social media provides a prism for understanding the political values held by social media users.

Key Trends and Topics in the Data

The patterns revealed by the analysis of the use of hashtags and the popularity level of users suggest a clear cleavage between Leave and Remain supporters before the referendum. However, hashtags and users in favour of Leave appeared to be much more popular than those supporting Remain. Take, the top 10 most popular hashtags and users, for example. Hashtags indicating Leave, such as #voteleave, were more popular than those suggesting Remain, such as #remain (Table 1.1). The top 10 most popular users in the tweets containing any of the top 10 most popular hashtags and those in all tweets were the same group of users, and they all supported Leave. @Stongerin – the Twitter handle of Britain Stronger in Europe, which was the official Remain campaign (The BBC, 2016) – only ranked as Top 16 in all pre-referendum tweets.

Table 1.2 shows the prominent topics identified in the analysis of key (meaningful) words in the tweets containing any of Leave or Remain hashtags. Apart from the topics of Leave, Remain and Referendum (neutral), topics, such as 'EU or related issues/countries', 'immigration' and 'the economy', suggest that the issues of immigration, the economy, regulation, democracy, sovereignty, security and the NHS were central to the concerns of users. The next section will present the findings from the qualitative analysis of selected tweets. These findings will interpret the meanings of these topics discovered in the computational analysisin more detail.

SOCIAL REPRESENTATIONS OF THE EU MEMBERSHIP ON TWITTER

The findings of the qualitative analysis match those trends and topics emerging from the computational analysis outlined above. They suggest that contrasting opinions about the referendum – Leave and Remain – were expressed on Twitter before (including) the referendum day. These views were linked with issues, such as democracy, immigration, the economy, the NHS and sovereignty, and resembled the main arguments of the Leave and Remain camps. These issues were connected with established concepts and concrete everyday objects, whose meanings were transferred to the idea of the EU membership through anchoring and objectification.

Leave

Anchoring of the EU Membership

The process of anchoring was outstanding in Leave tweets at the thematic and emotional levels. On the one hand, the EU membership was prominently connected with established and familiar concepts, such as democracy and freedom, and integrated into their established meaning systems. In particular, tweets promoting Leave adopted the dichotomy of 'democracy' versus 'dictatorship' and that of 'freedom' versus 'control' in describing the relationship between the

EU and the UK. The EU was labelled as a 'dictatorship'. An analogy was drawn between the UK's EU membership and sacrificing Britain's 'democracy' to the EU's 'dictatorship'. A small number of tweets even associated the EU with 'Nazi', 'Hitler' or 'Napoleon'. Hitler was a German politician and the leader of the Nazi Party. He was a dictator who started the Second World War in Europe by invading Poland. Napoleon was a French military leader who crowned himself emperor and attempted to invade Britain. Some tweets referred to the 'NaziOrigin' or 'Naziroots' of the EU. This association might trigger related historical memories of dictators in Europe. While the EU was portrayed as a dictatorship, being within the EU was seen to threaten the UK's democracy and to be identical to the UK giving in to the tyranny of the EU. This was exemplified in the following tweet (rephrased): I wish Britain will have a responsible #democracy again with #Voteleave #leaveEU #Brexit – the UK is not #strongerin under a #EU dictatorship @BrexitVoter (19 June 2016).

Likewise, Leave tweets extensively constructed oppositions between 'freedom'/'independence' and 'control' as well as between '(self-)control' and 'losing control'. Users in support of Leave cried to take back control in their tweets. Such tweets regarded that the EU membership had taken away freedom and independence from Britain. In this narrative, the UK's EU membership was described as an obstacle to Britain's control of domestic matters, such as borders, sovereignty, laws, finance and markets. Brussels was portrayed as being superior to Britain. A small number of tweets even associated the EU membership with 'slavery'.

On the other hand, the emotional anchor of 'hope' substantially appeared in Leave tweets, especially between 21 and 23 June 2016. These tweets dubbed the withdrawing from the EU 'Project Hope'. This naming strategy pictures the EU membership as something of the past, something old and broken, and something stopping Britain from developing in the future. It suggests getting rid of the EU membership and breaking down the status quo will give hope to the nation and the people of Britain. Brexit will be advantageous to the UK and beneficial, especially to children, as shown in the following tweet (rephrased): The main reason why we must vote leave is that we need to consider the future of our children in our nation #ProjectHope (21 June 2016).

The stark comparison between the emotional anchor of 'hope' and that of 'fear' constructed a dichotomy of 'hope' versus 'fear', as exemplified in the following tweet (rephrased): We need to believe in Britain and choose #ProjectHope over #ProjectFear. Let us vote to leave on #IndependenceDay (23 June 2016). The construction of this dichotomy contrasts the arguments and believes of the Leave and Remain camps, praising the Leave camp for bringing in 'hope' but accusing the Remain camp of creating 'fear'.

Tweets involving the use of the emotional anchor of 'fear' blamed Remainers for scaremongering about the potential economic consequences of Brexit. This naming tactic suggests that choosing to continue the EU membership embodies the elites' lack of confidence in the people and in the nation of Britain. It also shows as their giving in to the fear of the consequences of leaving the EU. This anchor once again implies the power of the EU in controlling the UK.

Additionally, the anchors of 'corruption' and 'incompetence' were used to justify the Leave arguments of users, which indicate their distrust of the current government and the ruling political elites. Leave tweets called David Cameron 'DodgyDave' who could not be trusted. They criticised the UK government and the Prime Minister for having lost Britain's global leadership. Remain politicians were accused of being 'unaccountable' and 'scaremongering' about the economic consequences of the Brexit vote. Sarcasm expressed in the tweets about Neil Kinnock also suggests an accusation of corruption against politicians.[1] Leave tweets also blamed David Cameron for supporting Turkey and Serbia to gain their EU membership, which had made the situation worse. They accused the then Prime Minister of facilitating EU enlargement, which had exaggerated the immigration problem faced by Britain. These anchors reflect the discourse of national populism, a characteristic of which is the corrupt (and incompetent) elite (Taggart, 2004).

Objectification of the EU Membership

The abstract concept of the EU membership is easier to process through being objectified into material and everyday objects, such as immigration and the NHS. As a result of objectification, its meanings have become closely linked with those of concrete objects.

Words or phrases in relation to immigration, such as 'immigration', 'migration', 'immigrant(s)', 'migrant(s)', 'refugee(s)', 'freedom of movement', 'free movement', 'right to travel' and 'mobility rights', were frequently mentioned. Voting to leave or remain in the EU was reduced to choosing between rejecting or welcoming immigration. Traditional stigmatising labels

1 Neil Kinnock is a senior Labour politician. Neil Kinnock and his wife Glenys Kinnock were involved in a £10 million scandal in the past.

often attached to immigrants, such as 'scrounging social benefits', were used to brand EU immigrants, although they came legally under Article 21. The EU membership was further objectified through association with issues perceived to be related to immigration, such as population growth, housing crisis, pressures on job markets and even threats to national security like terrorism.

The NHS was another prominent everyday object of objectification. The term of 'NHS' often appeared in tweets containing the hashtag: '#voteleave'. In a significant amount of Leave tweets, Brexit was portrayed as a panacea for the problems of the NHS – 'save the NHS'. The EU membership was regarded as an obstacle to the survival of the NHS in the UK, as exemplified by the following tweet (rephrased): please vote to Leave to save the NHS (23 June 2016). Leave supporters outlined three reasons why voting leave would mean saving the NHS. First, the EU took away the funding that was supposed to be used to support the NHS. Second, the EU membership would lead to the privatisation of the NHS. Third, being within the EU had prevented British people from securing medical jobs.

Most (16,320 out of 17,020) of the tweets containing the term of 'Brussels' also included the hashtag '#voteleave'. Leave tweets blamed Brussels for asking the UK for money and for controlling Britain through centralising law- and regulation-making. In particular, 'Brussels' was represented in tweets as an impediment to saving the NHS. Out of the 17,020 tweets mentioning the word of 'Brussels', 15,466 tweets (90.9%) also mentioned the term of 'NHS' at the same time. The following tweet sent by a UKIP MP John Douglas Wilson Carswell was representative: '#VoteLeave. I am with @Vote_leave because we should stop sending £350 million per week to Brussels, and spend our money on our NHS instead' (2 June 2016). It was the most retweeted tweet in the whole dataset, receiving 2,228 retweets. It was a typical example of tweets seeing 'Brussels' as a menace to the survival of the NHS. As a result of the anchoring and objectification of the EU membership, 'Brussels' became an icon in which the EU financially exploits the UK and politically prohibits the UK from exercising its sovereignty, protecting its national security and maintaining its robust public services.

To summarise, on Twitter, through anchoring and objectifying the EU membership, Leave supporters argued that the EU membership impaired the economy of the UK and took away job opportunities from Britons. Their arguments were mainly concerned with the economy and public services with an extra emphasis on nationalism and sovereignty. They dubbed leaving EU 'Project Hope' and the referendum day 'independenceday'. Users, supporting and advocating Leave, firmly demanded to 'take back control' and 'save your nation'.

Remain

Anchoring of the EU Membership

Remainers anchored the EU membership mostly at the thematic level. Two prominent themes emerged in tweets using the anchoring of the EU membership. First, the EU membership was prominently associated with stability, inclusion, security and prosperity. The first key concept that underpinned the arguments of Remainers was 'togetherness': remaining in the EU would make Britain a 'safer' and 'stronger' country while leaving the EU would leave Britain in 'isolation' and with 'uncertainty'. Although some tweets acknowledged the 'incompetence' of the EU, most of Remain tweets stressed the importance of 'stability', 'inclusion' and 'cooperation' to the future of Britain. The EU was viewed as essential for securing the global leadership of the UK. The EU membership was portrayed as a road leading to the success of Britain. The following tweet is representative (rephrased): I have sent postal vote for EU referendum. Although the EU may have its own problems, staying within the EU is still much better than Brexit, which would lead to uncertainty and isolation of Britain. #Remain (15 June 2016).

Second, the EU membership was anchored as a necessary restraint on the power of the British government and politicians. Interestingly, Remain tweets also criticised the British government and politicians – especially the Tory government, and Tory politicians like Boris Johnson and Michael Gove – for their ignorance, failures or 'lies' over issues, such as workers' rights, the NHS, the environment and taxation. In this regard, the EU membership was pictured as providing a much-needed check on British politics, as shown in the following tweet (rephrased): Do not trust Michael Gove and Boris Johnson with workers' rights. #StrongerIn #SaferIn (4 June 2016).

Objectification of the EU Membership

Like Leave tweets, Remain tweets objectified the EU membership into concrete and everyday objects similar to those in Leave tweets, such as immigration, the NHS, jobs and single market. However, the meanings conveyed through the association between the EU membership and these objects were absolutely different to those in Leave tweets. Remain tweets objectified the EU membership in favour of the Remain vote.

In Remain tweets, the objectification of the EU membership depicted the EU membership as being essential for the UK's economic stability and growth. It focused on the economy and public services, blaming Leave supporters for only caring about immigration but ignoring the economy. Take, the object of immigration, for example. Remain tweets showed an attempt to overthrow stigmatised images and meanings associated with immigrants by drawing attention to their positive contributions to the British economy and public services. On the one hand, these tweets interpreted immigration positively by recognising the contributions made by immigrants and migrants to the economy in the UK. On the other hand, they stressed the potential ramifications of the Brexit vote on the NHS workforce, a significant part of which was believed to have come from Europe, as exemplified in the following tweet (rephrased): Britain needs immigration. Twenty per cent of care workers come from outside the UK. Some 11% of the NHS workforce, including 26% of doctors, are non-UK. They are crucial. #Remain (13 June 2016).

With a focus on material and everyday objects, such as 'jobs', 'nurse shortage' and 'finance', the objectification of the EU membership in Remain tweets emphasised the potential negative impacts of Brexit on the economy, investment, jobs, wages, the NHS and trade, implying a bleak future for the UK. The single market, one of the most important objects closely linked with the EU membership in Remain tweets, symbolised the much-needed economic benefits of the EU membership for the UK.

CONCLUSION REMARKS

The research reported in this chapter shows that in their tweeting practices, users anchored and objectified the EU membership into material and everyday objects like the NHS and associated it with familiar concepts such as democracy. The processes of anchoring and objectification show that although echoing the respective arguments of the Leave and Remain political campaigns, Twitter users' understandings of the EU membership came from their everyday lives – established understandings of concepts and objects that they encountered every day. In so doing, the abstract political idea of the EU membership was given concrete meanings. This research offers a case for understanding the process of mass production of public opinion on political events on social media. This case particularly recognises the role played by contextually-embedded everyday objects and familiar concepts in producing and articulating the meanings of abstract political objects in everyday tweeting practices.

In this case, polarised collective meanings about the EU membership were expressed and forged on the platform of Twitter before the referendum, suggesting different political values and societal understandings of the UK-EU relationship. One understanding regarded the EU membership as a useful necessity for Britain's success, defending the established status quo of the UK-EU relationship, in particular, and in general the existing global geopolitical and economic orders. The opposite understanding, reflecting nationalist-populist perspectives, viewed the EU as being disastrous and problematic. The EU membership, thus, should be abandoned for the sake of the future of the UK. Meanwhile, the British government was seen as corrupt, lying and scaremongering. This societal understanding even drew on the historical memories of wars and dictators and social stigmas attached to immigration and extended them to interpret the relationship between the EU and the UK. This understanding of the EU membership contributed to the promotion of the values of national populism through challenging the established relationship between the EU and the UK and advocating withdrawing from the EU.

Such conflicting, collective meanings of the EU membership were made through the processes of anchoring and objectification on Twitter – either connecting the abstract idea of the EU membership with familiar concepts or objectifying it in to concrete everyday objects. These familiar concepts or specific everyday objects, such as immigration, the NHS, jobs and the economy, were the material reality faced by Twitter users in their everyday lives. Their everyday experiences and reflections on their everyday-life conditions formed 'social thinking' and 'collective cognitions' about the EU membership, which underpinned the social representations about it. This case confirms the importance of established, familiar concepts and everyday objects in producing and expressing public opinion about political objects through social media practice.

The research presented in this chapter shows that social media analysis can offer an alternative means to understand public opinion. In addition, social representations theory and the two mechanisms of anchoring and objectification can provide a useful analytical framework for analysing how collective meanings of the political object of the EU membership were created in communication on social media and in particular on Twitter. We, however, acknowledge the existence of two limitations of examining social media communication in order to understand social representations of objects. The first limitation is that we only can gain a static understanding of social representations, as discussed in the Introduction. Unless we will longitudinally monitor social media communication, we would not be able to understand the changes over time in social representations constructed on social media. In this case, for example, the analysis can merely offer a relatively static snapshot of the expression of social representations of the EU membership before the referendum rather than their dynamic development over a long time.

The second limitation is caused by the unknown identity of users and by the decontextualisation of their social media practices. Höijer (2011, p. 14) once pointed out social representations theory cannot really show the real 'practices and activities of people or groups of people when they are producing social representations'. This shortcoming of social representations theory is exacerbated by the uncertainty about the background of social media users, i.e. we lack the knowledge of who they were and in what context they used social media. Some scholars (see, for example, Bastos & Mercea, 2019; Howard & Kollanyi, 2016) even revealed the existence and effects of Twitterbots during the event. Echoing these arguments, this study contends that an analysis of social representations on Twitter would not reveal the detailed communication practices of users nor be able to accurately explain who these users are. The detailed practices and activities of social media users in producing social representations remain unknown to researchers unless they are examined by using traditional qualitative research methods like interviews or observation with them. The usefulness of these traditional research methods in social media studies may be worth exploring in the future. Besides, social media practices, such as 'retweet' and 'reply', would also influence the production of social representations of objects. Moreover, whether the limit of word length (up to 140 characters during the sampling time) would affect the meanings of Twitter posts is open to debate.

3

LEGITIMISING POLITICAL CONTROVERSY AND POPULISM

An ideology 'is a value or belief system that is accepted as fact or truth by some group. It is composed of sets of attitudes towards the various institutions and processes of society' (Sargent, 2009, p. 311). It is discursive and embodied in discourses (Hebdige, 2016). The domination of one ideology over others changes in tandem with the transformation of social dynamics. Once losing legitimacy, mainstream – or 'central' and 'dominant' in Raymond Williams' terms (Williams, 2016) – ideologies can drop to a marginal position. By contrast, 'marginal' ideologies can be accepted as part of the 'mainstream' after gaining legitimacy (Ang, 1991). In this process, the news media – and potentially the Internet and social media – play a crucial role in relation to legitimising deviant topics or views, which are usually excluded from or criticised in the media (Hallin, 1989). Uncritical salience in media coverage of these topics would allow them to achieve legitimacy and mainstream status.

The recent (re-)rise of populism is often seen as accompanying the surge in anti-globalisation sentiment and the crisis of globalisation (Cox, 2017; Cuperus, 2007; Milner, 2019; Peters, 2018). In the UK, the established discourses of globalisation and European integration have played a central role in shaping government policies since 1997 (Hay & Smith, 2005). British New Labour governments embraced globalisation and European integration, although there were calls for reform at the European level (Hay & Smith, 2005). However, later, along with the surfacing of more reservation about globalisation and European integration, post–New Labour governments paid more attention to social and environmental justice and the consequences of globalisation (Lynch, 2010).

Compared with the dominance of the globalisation and European integration discourses, populism was a marginal ideology in the last few decades. However, the UK, alongside other Western democratic societies, has recently experienced a spike in populism, which is demonstrated by the results of important political events such as referenda and elections (Alvares & Dahlgren, 2016; Krämer, 2017). The once marginal political ideology of populism has gradually found its way into mainstream political debates and is moving towards the centre. The news media are often blamed for mainstreaming populism and for legitimising the claims of populist politicians (Birenbaum & Villa, 2003; Mazzoleni, 2008). In light of the part played by the Internet, particularly social media, in facilitating the spread of populism (Engesser, Ernst, Esser, & Büchel, 2017; Postill, 2018), a question arises: whether and how do the online practices of users contribute to the mainstreaming of populism?

This chapter examines how the social media practices of British politicians and news media mainstreamed populism through the 2016 Brexit referendum debates on Twitter. Politicians, in particular, Nigel Farage, received enormous communicative freedom and extensive attention from ordinary Twitter users. The distinctive communicative style of his tweets conveyed a 'man on the street' tone, which enabled him to gain considerable popularity. The tweets of Boris Johnson echoed Farage's populist claims. Although expressing different viewpoints, Remain politicians did not criticise the populist claims made by Farage and Johnson. The lack of criticism justified and accepted populist claims as legitimate arguments about controversial issues surrounding the referendum.

Meanwhile, the news media paid overwhelming attention to politicians with a focus on the topics of immigration and the economy. The sphere of legitimate controversy was created, in which populist arguments were not only given the spotlight but also included as a legitimate part of the debates. Here, the Twitter practices of British politicians and of the news media led to the extensive – but largely uncritical – presence and articulation of populist claims alongside those of pro-European Union (EU) and pro-globalisation arguments. Such parallel articulation and presence mainstreamed these populist perspectives by giving them a central place in the debates about the referendum. The mainstreaming of populism on Twitter, however, is inextricably linked with, and thus needs to be understood within, the broader context of rising populism where the (once-)dominant ideologies of globalisation and European integration are in decline.

THE MEDIA, POPULIST POLITICIANS AND THE MAINSTREAMING OF POPULISM

In spite of being a contested ideological concept, populism is 'a communication phenomenon' (Vreese, Esser, Aalberg, Reinemann, & Stanyer, 2018). The news media has included populism in their coverage extensively but uncritically. They are blamed for legitimising and mainstreaming populism and thus facilitating its rise (Alvares & Dahlgren, 2016; Birenbaum & Villa, 2003; Rooduijn, 2014; Vreese et al., 2018; Waisbord, 2003). The European media, for example, were criticised for legitimising the claims of populist leaders (Mazzoleni, 2008). A 'supply and demand' relationship has been established between the news media – particularly the tabloid media – and populist leaders: 'the media, intentionally or not, may serve as powerful mobilisation tools for populist causes' (Mazzoleni, 2008, p. 50). Popularising populism through the news media is also exemplified in the case of Front National and Le Pen in France (Birenbaum & Villa, 2003) and the case of the UK Independence Party (UKIP) in the UK (Block & Negrine, 2017; Deacon & Wring, 2016).

Social change and issues, such as the 2007-2008 global financial crisis and the surge in populist public sentiment, are one explanation for the news media giving coverage to populism and populist politicians. An early example is that in the Danish context, social change – such as an increase in the number of refugees and the unemployment rate – was behind populism moving from being 'extreme to mainstream' in media coverage in the 1980s (Yılmaz, 2006). The communication style of populist politicians is another reason for why populism has received attention from the news media (Block & Negrine, 2017; Deacon & Wring, 2016). Populist parties and politicians have been found to have effective communicative and public relation strategies and performance styles (Deacon & Wring, 2016; Ekström, Patrona, & Thornborrow, 2018).

In recent years, the relationship between social media and populism has increasingly caught the interest of scholars (see, for example, Gerbaudo, 2018; Krämer, 2017; Postill, 2018). Social media sites offer a place where the people rally, form masses and speak out against partisan voices (Gerbaudo, 2018). Scholars argued that social media platforms supported the rise of 'populism 2.0' and right-wing populism (Gerbaudo, 2014, 2018; Krämer, 2017). With the popularity and pervasiveness of social media, populist discourses flourished on social platforms. While these studies are welcome, more research is needed to understand the role played by the media, and in particular social media, in spreading populism (Vreese et al., 2018).

Populist politicians, employing communication strategies, have been actively using not only the mainstream media but also omnipresent social media to promulgate their ideas among supporters (Bracciale & Martella, 2017; Engesser et al., 2017; Kreis, 2017; Zulianello, Albertini, & Ceccobelli, 2018). Beyond populist politicians, other politicians can also use social media to serve their respective interests and to disseminate their beliefs (Postill, 2018). The traditional news media have tried hard to maximise their own impact on social media. Following journalistic practices, they have sought to adapt their content (social media posts) to suit social platforms. For example, due to the word limit of Twitter, the news media have to keep their posts short, although traditional journalistic principles and routines still influence how journalists approach Twitter (Barnard, 2012; Lasorsa, 2012; Papacharissi & Easton, 2013). When politicians and the news media debate and 'compete' for attention on social media, would their social media practices contribute to mainstreaming populism? And if so, how does it happen?

The referendum case is an excellent one to address these questions for two reasons. Firstly, the division between Leave and Remain occurred within (rather than between) mainstream British political parties and among party leaders and members of Parliament (MPs) (Vasilopoulou, 2016), which suggests the support for populist values was not aligned with political parties' ideologies. Secondly, British news outlets officially declared their support for Remain or Leave before the referendum (Hobolt, 2016; Loughborough University, 2016). Their ideological inclinations and journalistic practices would thus influence their social media practices. In turn, this makes the role played by the social media practices of individual politicians and the news media in the spreading of populism particularly interesting.

FINDINGS

The analysis reveals that Twitter acted as an open forum where politicians expressed their respective views, and the news media adhered to routine journalistic practices. In general, the nine politician accounts were less active but more popular than the 13 media accounts.[1] Among the nine politician accounts, Remainer @David_Cameron was the most active, sending out 178 messages (see Fig. 3.1).[2] However, Brexiteers @Nigel_Farage and @BorisJohnson were the

1 When approaching the referendum day, especially from 16 June 2016, the original tweets of the news media received more retweets than those of politicians. However, we still considered politicians more popular than the news media on Twitter, because the news media sent out original tweets ten or even a hundred times more than politicians.

2 Although David Cameron was reportedly Eurosceptic in the past, he was categorised as a 'Remainer' according to his attitude towards the referendum at the time of the referendum.

most popular. The two groups – politicians and the news media – rarely retweeted each other's tweets. An apparent difference between politicians and the news media was that politicians clarified their opinions in tweets. By contrast, most tweets of the news media were fact-based or cited news sources. Including opposing viewpoints in the tweets of the two groups presents populist arguments alongside those supporting globalisation and the EU.

Tweeting Practices of Politicians

Politicians tweeted about the referendum in support of campaign goals. Their tweets displayed their attitudes towards the referendum and constructed arguments with ideological implications. Not only Nigel Farage, the then leader of the populist UKIP, but also Boris Johnson of the Conservative Party, who became the Prime Minister in the UK three years later (in 2019), made populist claims in their tweets. Notably, while Nigel Farage sharply criticised David Cameron in his tweets, his and Boris Johnson's arguments did not receive significant criticism from politicians who tweeted in favour of globalisation and remaining in the EU. Farage and Johnson were extremely popular on Twitter, whose popularity levels were higher than those of most media accounts (Fig. 3.1). Their tweets were populist and emotional, encouraging people to vote to leave the EU to change the status quo, to protect the sovereignty of the UK and to shield the interests of locals.

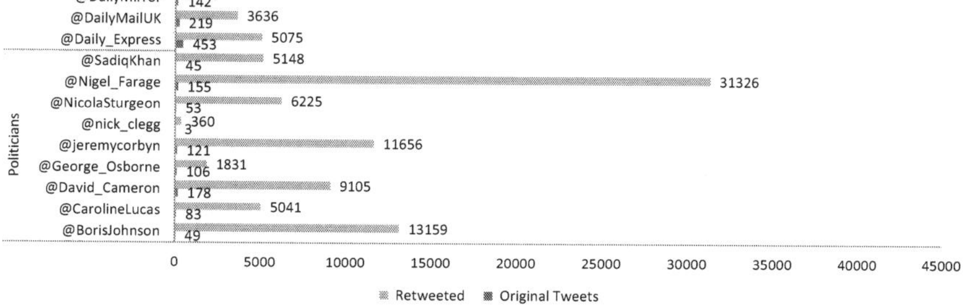

Fig. 3.1. The Numbers of Original Tweets Sent by Nine Politician and Thirteen News Media Twitter Accounts and the Numbers of Retweets They Received before (and on) the Referendum Day (y-axis: Politician and Media Accounts; X-axis: Number of Tweets).

The 155 original tweets of @Nigel_Farage aimed to mobilise local populations and promulgate the nationalist-populist arguments of the Leave campaign. His tweets, speaking on behalf of the people against the elites, took the people's side, as exemplified in the tweet: 'People in Bolton sick of establishment scare tactics. They want to Leave EU & get their country back #BrexitBusTour https://t.co/BuBT5eJT4C' (25 May 2016). His accessible writing style and 'man on the street' tone distinguish his tweets from those of other politicians. He advocated Brexit to take back control. 'Back Brexit', 'take back control' and 'immigration' were the three main themes identifiable in his tweets. The most prominent argument was that we should vote to leave to take back control, control borders and regain our independence and sovereignty, as exemplified in the tweet: 'UK could do so much better as an independent, self-governing nation. Vote to Leave on June 23rd. https://t.co/d2bPkCnEOY' (6 June 2016).

Nigel Farage also argued that if we do not curb immigration, including free movement and illegal immigrants, our population will explode and damage our public services, education and housing. He complained about Britain's high financial costs of its EU membership, which also hurts the local fishing industry, local business and the interests of residents. Celebrating the support of mainstream politicians, such as Boris Johnson, Farage accused Remainers, such as David Cameron and the government, of being wrong and lying. He harshly criticised the EU for being bossy and disastrous and accused the UK of having helped Turkey to achieve EU membership, as exemplified in the tweet 'Turkey and others are to receive funding from the UK to help those countries prepare for full EU membership!' (19 June 2016).

Most of his tweets were his own comments. Occasionally citing academic views and mentioning historical events such as the Battle of the Somme, Nigel Farage compared the referendum to a battle against the invasion of the EU and a fight for the freedom of the British nation. This historical reference could trigger voters' patriotism and nationalism. The following tweet is representative: 'We remember the Battle of Jutland 100 years ago today and the huge sacrifices made for our freedom' (31 May 2016).

Despite being less emotional than those of @Nigel_Farage, the 49 original messages of @BorisJohnson were still nationalist and populist. His main arguments focused on immigration and the economy, for example, concerning the financial costs of EU membership. He called to take back control and dubbed the referendum day 'Independence Day'. He rejected the arguments of big businesses and economists who said that the Brexit vote would have damaging economic consequences. He 'stood up' to the elites by accusing big corporations and elites of being 'wrong'. One of his messages, for example, referred to a 1981 statement as an 'attack' on Mrs Thatcher, the then Prime Minister, suggesting economists could make mistakes: 'And remember the 364 economists inc two Nobel prize winners who attacked Mrs T in 1981 #VoteLeave #InOrOut' (3 June 2016). The arguments of Boris Johnson, which criticised the elites and supported leave, are a substantial addition to the populist arguments of Nigel Farage.

In the virtual space of Twitter, the populist claims of @Nigel_Farage and @BorisJohnson confronted the arguments of the other seven Remain politicians.[3] The latter's arguments were more rational and pro-Europe, reflected the perspectives of the elites and focused on the issues of economic prosperity, stability and security. Supporting globalisation and European integration, they advocated Remain and defended the UK-EU relationship and EU membership. However, they did not directly criticise or confront the arguments put forward by Nigel Farage or Boris Johnson on Twitter.

Consider, for example, the tweets of @David_Cameron and @jeremycorbyn.[4] The 178 original tweets of @David_Cameron advocated 'vote remain' and 'stronger in', for the sake of the economy, security, the National Health Service (NHS), younger generations and Britain's global leadership and opportunities. Jobs, businesses, prices and shops were among the main issues concerning the economy. He warned that voting to leave is 'irreversible', risky and with no way back. He also mentioned several times the environmental consequences of the Brexit vote. The phrase of 'Stronger, safer and better off' repeatedly appeared in his tweets. He, however, almost completely ignored Nigel Farage. His only criticism of Farage can be found in a tweet requesting that 'we shouldn't take a leap in the dark with Nigel Farage' (7 June 2016). Cameron relied on the opinions of experts to explain why leaving the EU would be a disaster for the economy. These experts were members of the elites supporting the existing global economic order and the UK's EU membership. The following tweet is representative: 'We should listen to experts when they warn us of the dangers to our economy of leaving the European Union' (16 June 2016). Overall, his tweets were rational, relying on the perspective of the elites and echoing the logic of globalisation and European integration. They were diametrically opposed to the emotional and populist tweets of Nigel Farage.

---

3 The other seven Remain politicians were categorised as 'Remainers' because of their attitudes to the referendum at the time of the referendum.

4 Jeremy Corbyn's previous stance towards remaining in the EU was not clear, as shown in his 'seven out of 10' statement on the EU. Despite so, he was classified as a 'Remainer' for his attitude towards the referendum at the time of the referendum.

Likewise, Jeremy Corbyn's tweets also reflected the perspectives of the elites and supported the idea of European integration. His arguments, however, resonated with the narratives of the previous New Labour government, which believed reforms were needed at the European level. His tweets spoke from the perspectives of the Labour leader and 'trade union leaders' rather than the people or workers. @jeremycorbyn supported Remain, stressing the benefits of Britain's EU membership. However, he criticised the current Tory government. His tweets served the interests of the Labour Party. His arguments mainly focused on the rights of workers, the NHS and jobs, blaming the Tories for neglecting these issues. Corbyn repeatedly mentioned the views of trade union leaders and expressed his dream of establishing 'a real social Europe', calling for reform in the EU. He also advocated rejecting the politics of 'fear', implying populist politicians were playing the 'fear' card and were using the fear of immigrants as a political weapon in the campaign. However, he did not speak from the perspective of the people. Additionally, he completely neglected Nigel Farage and Boris Johnson, neither denouncing nor responding to their arguments.

The way in which the nine British politicians used Twitter and the content of their tweets show that Twitter offered them a forum where they were able to articulate their positions with respective ideological inclinations. The massive popularity of politicians on Twitter means a wide circulation of their messages, promoting their embodied ideological components. Populist claims made by both Nigel Farage and Boris Johnson were presented as part of the political arguments about the controversial referendum. In particular, the communicative style of Nigel Farage was much more accessible than that of Remain politicians. The articulation, but lack of criticism, of populist arguments, appearing alongside other political arguments, thereby legitimised and mainstreamed them in the debates about the referendum.

Tweeting Practices of the News Media

The analysis reveals that the news media adhered to journalistic practices on Twitter, exemplified by their use of traditional news sources. Cited as primary news sources, politicians – including those holding populist claims such as Nigel Farage and Boris Johnson – were given extensive attention and publicity. As a result, the news media's tweets (referred to as 'media tweets' in the remainder of the chapter) included, elaborated and evolved the position statements of politicians into two sides of legitimate debates about the referendum. All Twitter accounts of the news media cited spoken news sources from both sides of the discussions about the referendum. The majority of spoken news sources were economic, political or cultural elites – either individuals or institutions. The most prominent type of spoken news sources was 'Politicians' with 643 occurrences, accounting for 65.3% of all 985 spoken news sources. Prohibited by the word limit of Twitter, the news media seldom explained why and how for these statements in their tweets, although they often included links to reports containing relevant, more detailed analysis. Consequently, these tweets merely presented different viewpoints – as 'he said, and she said', ping-pong journalism without offering meaningful stories or critical analysis.

Overall, media tweets gave most attention to David Cameron and Nigel Farage as news sources and news actors. For example, David Cameron, the most quoted politician, was cited 121 times as a spoken news source, followed by Nigel Farage and Jeremy Corbyn (64 and 59 times, respectively). Cameron and Farage were also most frequently mentioned in media tweets as news actors. Boris Johnson and Michael Gove were also among the most frequently quoted spoken news sources (47 and 45 times, respectively). However, Nick Clegg and Caroline Lucas, key politicians for the Liberal Democrats and the Green Party, rarely received attention. Moreover, a detailed analysis of the stances of the politicians quoted reveals a clear division between Leave and Remain (Fig. 3.2), indexing the controversy constructed by politicians with opposing views about the referendum.

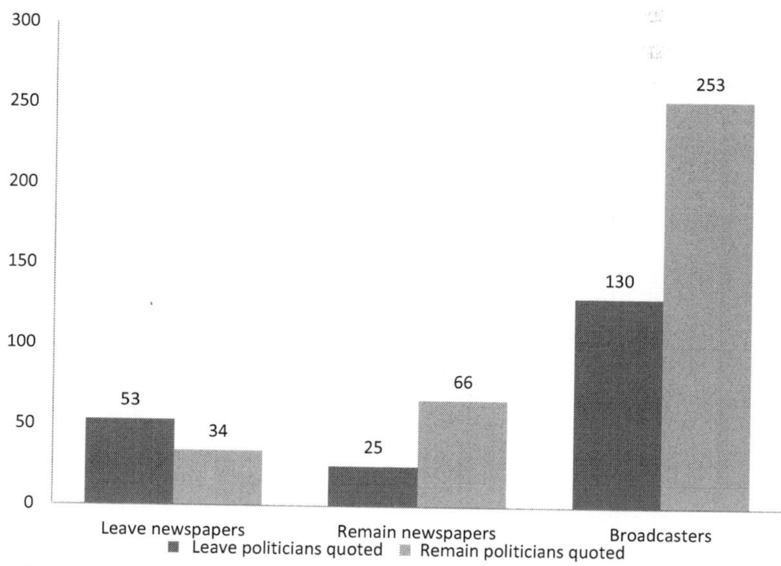

Fig. 3.2. Referendum Stances of Politician Spoken News Sources Quoted by the News Media in Their Tweets.

Media tweets constructed two primary agendas – immigration and the economy, ahead of other minor topic areas, such as public services, sovereignty, independence and institutional reform. Media tweets also interpreted the aforementioned contested political arguments made by politician news sources. The ideological stances of the news media influenced the interpretation of these agendas and the meaning of politicians' arguments. The issue of immigration, for example, was most prominent in the tweets of right-wing Leave newspapers: @DailyMailUK, @Daily_Express and @TheSun. The arguments constructed in their tweets justified the populist claims made by Nigel Farage and others. Although citing both sides of the arguments, these tweets of right-wing Leave newspapers advocated anti-immigration voices. They associated immigration with 'public fear' and the perceived 'migrant crisis', stressing the tragedies of migrants trying to cross the Channel and highlighting the flow of 'illegal' migrants 'sneaking' into the UK, the criminal activities of immigrants and the perceived need to curb immigration. In relation to the concerns about free movement, their tweets reported on the 'public fear' and pressure triggered by the 'influx' of migrants on the population, housing, public services and jobs in Britain. They implied that the current government and the UK's EU membership would lead to the arrival of more migrants. Opinions cited in the tweets of Leave newspapers, such as @TheSun and @Telegraph, blamed Cameron for his ignorance of the 'influx' of migrants and accused Remain elites, such as Cameron and Osborne, of being 'too rich to understand mass migration fears'. By contrast, they treated Nigel Farage favourably and uncritically. The tweets of @TheSun, for example, constructed an image of illegal immigrants by citing words of political elites like Nigel Farage as exemplified in the following tweet: '"We will have migrant bodies on UK beaches if we remain in the EU": Nigel Farage's warning https://t.co/YPGPsabyol https://t.co/prljcL2n8b' (4 June 2016). Right-wing Leave newspapers' tweets about immigration thus interpreted and justified the populist arguments about immigration made by Nigel Farage and Boris Johnson but refuted those by Remain politicians such as David Cameron.

'Immigration' was also prominent in the tweets of Remain newspapers, in particular, @guardian and @independent. The content of their tweets about immigration defended the 'free movement of people', outlined the contribution made by immigrants to British society and the economy and differentiated EU immigration from illegal immigration. @guardian, for example, quoted politicians such as David Cameron, Jeremy Corbyn and Gordon Brown, who argued that Brexit would not help immigration and the 'real problem' was 'illegal' immigration. Likewise, @independent cited politicians such as Angela Eagle and Ed Miliband, who argued EU immigration had been used as an 'alibi' for problems such as the NHS crisis by Brexit campaigners, such as Nigel Farage, and who regarded immigration as essential and a good thing to the UK. The Leave and Remain newspapers thus constructed two opposing discourses in their tweets, respectively, supporting populism and European integration.

The tweets of broadcasters cited both sides of arguments in relation to immigration. The majority (about 65%) of the immigration tweets of @SkyNews, for example, reflected the viewpoints of Brexiteers, particularly Nigel Farage, concerning immigration on the grounds of a growing number of immigrants, illegal migrants and the EU's power over the UK's home immigration policies. However, some 20% of the tweets did mention that migrant workers should not be blamed and Brexit would not change immigration but would damage the economy and the economic contribution of immigrants. Broadcasters' tweets about immigration juxtaposed populist arguments against pro-Europe arguments. Such juxtaposition constructs them as legitimate arguments in debates about controversial issues regarding the referendum.

Media tweets about the economy had similar effects. In tweets about the economy, broadcasters and Remain newspapers cited political and economic elites – including individuals and organisations – who were warning of the negative economic consequences of Brexit. Prominent among them are George Osborne, '10 labour city leaders', the 'IMF', 'French economy minister', 'US Federal Reserve chairwoman Janet Yellen' and the 'Bank of England'. Their tweets also quoted the elite members who accused Leave politicians, such as Boris Johnson, of telling lies and being untruthful and criticised Brexiteers for ignoring the disastrous economic consequences of Brexit. By contrast, the tweets of Leave newspapers supported populist arguments by uncritically covering more messages from Brexiteers such as Nigel Farage and Boris Johnson. They also criticised Remainers for 'scaremongering' about the economy.

In these ways, the populist claims of Leave politicians, and in particular, Nigel Farage and Boris Johnson, were put under the spotlight in media tweets and mainstreamed as a legitimate element of debates about the referendum.

DISCUSSION AND CONCLUSION

The findings in this study echo the views of other scholars about the role played by social media in facilitating the rise of populism (see, for example, Engesser et al., 2017; Postill, 2018). It is also well understood that politicians use Twitter to gain a (perceived and/or real) political advantage (Golbeck,

Grimes, & Rogers, 2010; Graham, Broersma, Hazelhoff, & Haar, 2013; Grant, Moon, & Grant, 2010; Jackson & Lilleker, 2011; Rauchfleisch & Metag, 2016). The research presented in this chapter demonstrates the importance of the tweeting practices of politicians and the news media in creating a sphere of legitimate controversy where populist claims were mainstreamed into legitimate political debates. In a time when populist values are no longer always attached to the ideologies of political parties, how individual politicians promulgate or denounce them becomes crucial. As shown in this research, while Leave politicians uttered their populist arguments in an accessible style, Remain politicians were uncritical of these populist statements. Instead, they focused on expressing their opinions from the perspectives of the pro-EU and pro-globalisation elites, addressing their own or own party's political interests. The articulation of populist arguments by Leave politicians, receiving no criticism from Remain politicians (on Twitter), places them at one side of the debates about the referendum, with Remain politicians' arguments on the other.

Politicians also exerted influence when the news media extensively, although uncritically, cited their arguments in media tweets. The tweeting practices of the news media were in accordance with journalistic practices and influenced by the news media's stances towards the referendum. In particular, in the tweets of the right-wing Leave newspapers, uncritically and favourably quoting populist politicians such as Nigel Farage would give legitimacy to these politicians and their populist claims. Giving voices to both Leave and Remain politicians and focusing on the issues of immigration and the economy, the tweets of the news media presented populist views in parallel with the arguments supporting European Integration and globalisation – which were made from the perspectives of established elites. They thus constructed the sphere of legitimate controversy allowing populist arguments to become part of the political debates. What is striking, in this case, is the role played by the tweeting practices of individual politicians and the news media in conveying opposing ideologies and including populist arguments into legitimate debates. In this way, mainstreamed and legitimised populism came to occupy a central place in the political debates surrounding the Brexit referendum.

Social media communication about populism should be seen 'as part of a larger information system' (Vreese et al., 2018, p. 432). The mainstreaming of populism on Twitter mirrors the emergence of populism and the decline in the dominance and establishment of globalisation and Europe integration in context. Prior to the referendum, British society witnessed a surge in Euroscepticism, as a significant part of the population blamed immigration and globalisation for their own situation and economic standing. Populist politicians used rising Euro-scepticism to gain a foothold in politics. Often, the more aberrant remarks they make, the more attention they would receive, and the better they would enthuse their supporters. Notably, embracing public sentiment is no longer limited to UKIP politicians, but an appealing strategy to politicians from all political parties. The debate about the UK's EU membership had moved 'from the margins to the mainstream of British politic', as part of 'the mainstreaming of Euro-scepticism in the UK', and British news media, in particular the tabloids, were the vital driving force behind it (Startin, 2015). The right-wing news outlets such as The *Daily Telegraph* and *The Sun* have represented (and even stirred up) the rising sentiment of Euro-scepticism. They have been facilitating the discussion of populism by continuously focusing on issues like immigration and by 'othering' non-national migrants (Tong & Zuo, 2019), which is consistent with the findings of this study. Populist politicians, such as Nigel Farage, have received extensive media coverage and have created a symbiotic relationship with the media (Block & Negrine, 2017; Deacon & Wring, 2016). The *Mail*, for example, portrayed Nigel Farage as 'a man on a mission' and as a 'hero' (Kelsey, 2016, p. 971).

The degree to which populism is a welcome feature of the contemporary political landscape is open to debate and discussion, and the actions of the news media cannot be seen as the only explanatory factor in the rise of populism. Populist parties across Europe have achieved successive electoral victories, many of which predate the extensive use of social media, and are the result of carefully constructed communication and public relation strategies (Deacon & Wring, 2016). There is also no homogeneity in the news media. The level of publicity received by populist political actors in media coverage is subject to journalistic principles and practices, which involves careful analysis and critique. What is more, populist arguments put forward by right-wing newspapers might be challenged by left-wing newspapers and political actors holding different political values. Also notable is that politicians using the tools offered to them by social media platforms do not have to rely on the news media to get their messages across to the public and are thus able to communicate directly with large numbers of citizens. Clearly, populist discourses thrive more easily on social media platforms, where the gate-keeping role of the news media is absent, and right-wing populist politicians have mastered the affordances of social media to propagate their populist ideas actively.

This line of argument suggests that the (relatively) free flow of information on social media platforms is a precondition for spreading populist values (Figenschou & Beyer, 2014; Figenschou & Ihlebæk, 2019; Figenschou & Thorbjørnsrud, 2017). More important, however, is social media's potential to mainstream populist values into political debates about controversial issues in the sphere of legitimacy controversy. By being included in political debates, deviant political values gain the status of legitimacy and are pushed towards the centre. In this research, whilst Remain politicians were successful in promoting their own values on social media, they failed to denounce populist values as deviant. This suggests a fatal misunderstanding by the Remain camp of the way in which Twitter works in shaping political discourse. It also points to Twitter as an alternative 'virtual' sphere where different views are expressed and evolve to form the basis of legitimate debates in the public domain. Adhering to journalistic practices, such as citing news sources and researching the validity of statements and claims, becomes a hindrance in the Twittersphere, and in the case presented here, it resulted in populist statements going unchallenged.

This chapter explores the social media practices of British politicians and the news media when communicating about the UK's EU referendum in 2016. It shows how the Twitter practices of the two groups resulted in the mainstreaming of the populist ideology by including populist claims within the boundaries of legitimate debates about the referendum.

4

THE CONSTRUCTION OF 'HERO' VERSUS 'VILLAIN' IN TWITTER USERS' RESPONSES TO @DAVID_CAMERON AND @NIGEL_FARAGE

Social media research has established the theory of political homophily – and that of the effects of 'echo chambers' – in regard to the social media practices of users. Derived from the sociological and social psychological domains, the concept of political homophily refers to the tendency of people to connect with others who are politically alike (Gerber, Henry, & Lubell, 2013; Huber & Malhotra, 2017; McPherson, Smith-Lovin, & Cook., 2001). This theory regards political agreement as playing a vital role in shaping the expression of users and their connections and interactions with the others on social media platforms. It argues that social media users choose to expose to information that supports, rather than challenges, their own views, and they would like to interact with other like-minded users. Such practices may result in the formation of political 'echo chambers' where users are politically homogenous – sharing the same ideologies or holding similar political values. This theory, however, has been criticised of being 'over-stated' (Dubois & Blank, 2018) and overestimating 'ideological segregation' (Barberá, Jost, Nagler, Tucker, & Bonneau, 2015).

Guided by the research tradition on political homophily, this chapter investigates how Twitter users responded to David Cameron and Nigel Farage, who were on opposing sides of the debate about the Brexit referendum. In particular, it examines the attitudinally selective exposure of Twitter users: (1) whether and the extent to which they were supportive of the politician whose tweets they heavily retweeted or whom they extensively mentioned in their tweets, and (2) what they discussed about the politician.

In the run-up to the referendum, David Cameron enthusiastically advocated Remain, whilst Nigel Farage endeavoured to achieve the Brexit vote. Both of them (@David_Cameron and @Nigel_Farage) were active on Twitter promoting their respective stances and arguments. An understanding of how Twitter users responded to the two politicians can advance our knowledge of the role played by shared views and political disagreement of users – in particular, Leave and Remain supporters in this case – in shaping the political discourse of the referendum on social media. The mixed-method analysis of the social networks and topics surrounding @David_Cameron and @Nigel_Farage in Twitter communication about the referendum in one month leading up to the event has enabled us to gain such an understanding. The analysis shows that the core social networks surrounding the two politicians' twitter handles were ideologically divided. In these networks, Leave users noticeably outnumbered Remain users. The content analysis – a combination of qualitative analysis of the tweets of the key users in these core networks and computational topic modelling of the tweets that mentioned either of the twitter handles of two politicians – suggests that @David_Cameron was under siege by Brexit supporters. By contrast, most of the users who extensively retweeted or mentioned @Nigel_Farage supported and praised him as a hero and saviour of British democracy.

The research reported in this chapter shows the importance of the ideological orientations of users in social media communication. In this case, in spite of the evident presence of political polarisation and homophily, political disagreement between Leave users and David Cameron was noticeably underlying the tweeting practices of the former. Leave users retweeted the tweets of @David_Cameron to express their disagreement – rather than their support for him. Their responses to @David_Cameron denounced and delegitimised the then Prime Minister and the values and ideology of the Remain campaign that he supported. Leave users were much more active than Remain users in speaking out their voices and in fiercely criticising and confronting the different values and ideology in the Twitter-sphere before the referendum. In this case, not only ideological homophily but also ideological antagonism and confrontation were manifested on Twitter. The study contributes to the current literature on political homophily and social media communication.

SOCIAL MEDIA AND POLITICAL HOMOPHILY

Political homophily, referring to 'the tendency to form connections with others who are politically similar' (Gerber et al., 2013, p. 598), has been a focus of political communication research. Existing research suggests that individuals and groups would like to choose to consume information with similar values and to communicate and interact with those with shared ideologies and beliefs. Instead, it is less likely for them to select to expose to diverse – or opposite – viewpoints. In so doing, they diminish 'cognitive dissonance', form homogeneous groups, and associate with those who share the same views or ideologies (Colleoni, Rozza, & Arvidsson, 2014; Festinger, 1954, 1957; Huckfeldt & Sprague, 2006; McPherson & Smith-Lovin, 1987; Sears & Freedman, 1967). Scholars warned that these communication behaviours would create the echo chamber effect that may lead to political and group polarisation and segmentation in society (Festinger, 1954; Jamieson & Cappella, 2008; Sunstein, 2009). The 'echo chamber' effect suggests that information exchange among like-minded users may reinforce their existing opinions and thus facilitate the formation and spread of political homophily and polarisation on the Internet.

Studies about communication and participation on the Internet in general, and in particular social media, also detected the existence of political homophily and that of echo chambers (Bright, 2018; Colleoni et al., 2014; Garrett, 2009a; Gilbert, Bergstrom, & Karahalios, 2009; Goldie, Linick, Jabbar, & Lubienski, 2014; Gorodnichenko, Pham, & Talavera., 2018). For example, in the run-up to the UK's 2010 general election, Liberal Democrat's Facebook users were found to have been Nick Clegg's supporters. This means that the political discussions on the social site took place among these users who were 'within a "Liberal Democrat echo chamber"' (Harris & Harrigan, 2015, p. 262). Filtering algorithms were used automatically or by users to filter out content containing political disagreement (Flaxman, Goel, & Rao, 2013; Pariser, 2011; Sunstein, 2009). Users were found avoiding – or 'shielding' – themselves from different views (Zhu, Skoric, & Shen, 2017).

As critics have pointed out, the level of political homophily, however, may vary from individuals to individuals and from groups to groups (Boutyline & Willer, 2017). Thus, we need to pay attention to users' actual social media use and practices. For example, a study examining the political content shared on Twitter by the Democrats and Republicans in the United States (US) found that the Republicans displayed higher levels of political homophily than that of the Democrats did. Therefore, the researchers suggested 'research on political homophily on the Internet should take the political culture and practices of users seriously' (Colleoni et al., 2014, p. 317).

Other scholars shifted their focus from political homophily to the role played by disagreement and opposition in political communication and participation. Conflicts and disagreement are seen as unavoidable in politics (Klofstad,

Sokhey, & McClurg, 2012). Political disagreement takes place when people confront political viewpoints that differ from their own (Huckfeldt, Johnson, & Sprague, 2004; Mutz, 2006; Smithson & Vraga, 2017). However, some scholars argued that individuals would 'reassess their positions' if they encounter different views (Huckfeldt & Sprague, 2006, p. 20).

Some studies found evidence of user exposure to political disagreement on the Internet. Online and social media users do not necessarily avoid different opinions and may be exposed to ideologically and politically diverse information (Bakshy, Messing, & Adamic, 2015; Garrett, 2009b; Messing & Westwood, 2014). The more users engage with 'news and current affairs' content, the more likely they are exposed to political disagreement (Yang, Barnidge, & Rojas, 2017, p. 27). However, the stronger the political ideologies users have, the less tolerant they are of political disagreement (Yang et al., 2017). On social media, even without interactions, users may still experience disagreement (Schulz & Roessler, 2012). The offline experiences of users are also crucial in shaping their information exposure on the Internet (Vaccari et al., 2016).

As discussed earlier in this book, the outcome of the UK's EU membership referendum – 52% Leave versus 48% Remain – is an expression of profound political and ideological divisions in British society (Ford & Goodwin, 2017; Goodwin & Heath, 2016; Iakhnis, Rathbun, Reifler, & Scotto, 2018). The UKIP, led by Nigel Farage at the time of the referendum, is believed to have played a crucial part in the Leave campaign, potently influencing the vote outcome (Goodwin & Heath, 2016; Iakhnis et al., 2018). The debate before the referendum happened between the Leave and Remain camps. These show the referendum is an excellent case study to examine whether, how, and the extent to which, shared views and political disagreement can shape political debates on the Internet in general, and social media in particular.

To address this question, we chose to focus on examining Twitter users' responses to David Cameron (@David_Cameron) and Nigel Farage (@Nigel_Farage). These two politicians were key figures in the Remain and Leave camps. David Cameron promised the referendum and strongly advocated Remain. Nigel Farage had been promoting the idea of leaving the EU and the 'independence' of the UK. Following the discussion in the existing literature on shared views and political disagreement, we wanted to answer the following two questions in this study reported in this chapter:

(1) Whether, and to what extent, were the core networks surrounding the twitter handles of David Cameron and Nigel Farage supportive networks?

(2) What views did Twitter users, who extensively retweeted or mentioned David Cameron and/or Nigel Farage, hold about (either or both of) the two politicians?

FINDINGS

The existing literature suggests that British politicians may not excel at using social media. For example, a study comparing the social media use by American and British politicians argued British politicians overall had an 'ineffective use of new technologies' and missed out on the opportunities provided by social media to engage voters in the run-up to the 2010 election (Harris & Harrigan, 2015, p. 262). However, the present study reported in this book has found that both David Cameron and Nigel Farage were active and very popular during the sampling time. In particular, Nigel Farage was vocal and persuasive in stating his Brexit and populist claims and in criticising David Cameron and the Remain campaign.

Overall, the social media practices of Twitter users presented clear evidence of the presence of both political homophily and ideological confrontation, particularly notably in Pro-Brexit tweets. However, intricate patterns were found in the responses of users to the two politicians. Their responses were far from being as simple as Leave users responding – either retweeting or mentioning – to Nigel Farage and Remain users responding to David Cameron. Generally, Leave users were more active in responding to both politicians than Remain users. More supportive topics and themes were detected in Leave users' responses to Nigel Farage. By contrast, David Cameron received much more criticism and confrontation from Leave users.

Research question one asks about the nature of social networks surrounding @David_Cameron and @Nigel_Farage. Research question two explores the attitudes of Twitter users towards the two politicians when they retweeted the latter's tweets or mentioned either @David_Cameron or @Nigel_Farage. The answers to these questions vary between the two handles.

Social Network Analysis and Qualitative Thematic Analysis

This study examined the retweet-based networks among users (see a more detailed discussion in Tong & Zuo, 2018). The core social networks surrounding @David_Cameron were found to be oppositional. That is to say, most of the key users in his core networks disagreed with David Cameron in relation to the referendum. However, @Nigel_Farage was clearly in supportive networks, which means that most of the key users in his core networks shared the same Brexit views as him. The tweets sent from both handles were heavily retweeted by Brexit supporters. In the core networks surrounding the two handles, Brexit users dominantly outnumbered Remain users (see Fig. 4.1). All users in core networks retweeted more than 30 times. In Fig. 4.1, each node represents a Twitter account, and each edge resembles a retweeting relationship between two accounts (see more discussions in Tong & Zuo, 2018). The width of an edge (in Fig. 4.1) shows the level of retweeting interactions between two accounts connected by the edge, while the size of a node indicates the activity

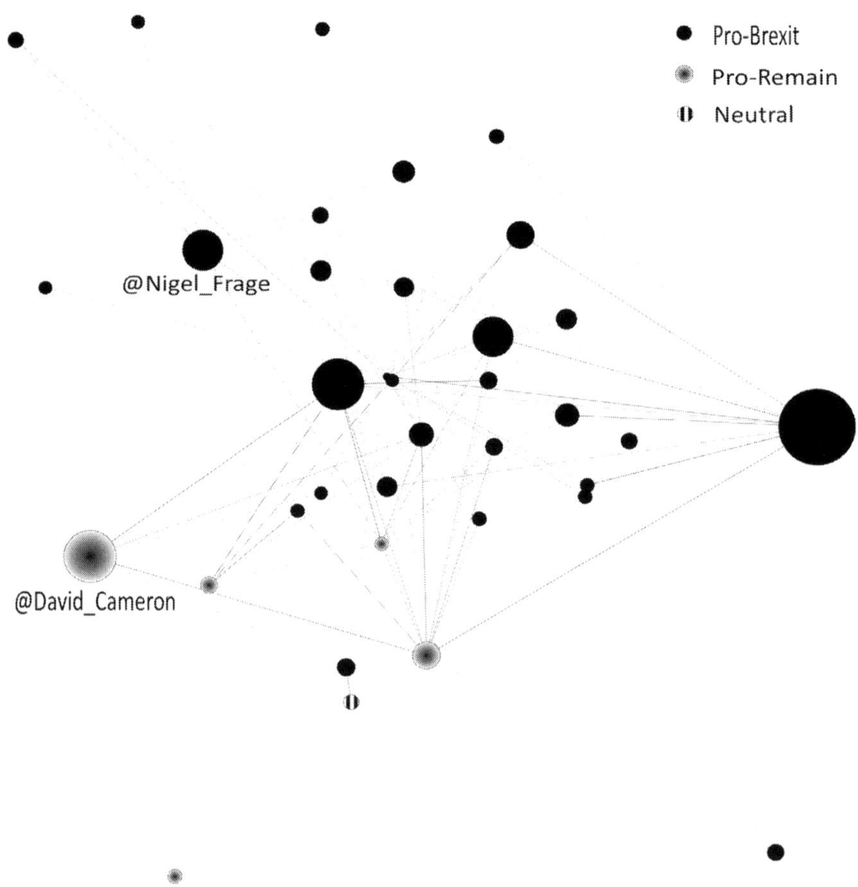

Fig. 4.1. Core Networks Surrounding @David_Cameron and @Nigel_Farage (Solid Black: pro-Brexit; Gradual Grey: pro-Remain; Stripy: Neutral).

level of the node. The thicker an edge was, the more retweets there were between the two accounts connected by the edge. The bigger a node was, the more tweets were posted or retweeted by the account.

Overall, the key users in the core networks surrounding the two politicians clearly supported one politician but strongly criticised the other. The majority of the key users (seven out of eight users) in @David_Cameron's core networks were pro-Brexit. Their tweets were largely (negatively) emotional in style and lacked reasonable arguments. They clearly expressed their pro-Brexit viewpoints and were disapproval of David Cameron and his Remain supporters. Some tweets even contained verbal abuse and emotional attacks against him. The seven themes (see Table 4.1) revealed in the qualitative thematic analysis of their tweets suggest these tweets criticised, denounced and delegitimised David Cameron and his Remain arguments. David Cameron was as much seen as a failure and loser as Nigel Farage was hailed as a hero and winner by the key users in David Cameron's core networks, exemplified in this tweet (rephrased): Michael Gove kicked hard the ass of @David_Cameron this week. @Nigel_Farage will demolish you next week! YUMMY!! #InOrOut #VoteLeave (3 June 2016).

Only one key user (@StrongerIn) in @David_Cameron's core networks supported Remain and David Cameron but meanwhile criticised the Leave campaign. For example, while adoring David Cameron's performance in TV debates for making 'a passionate case for why we're better off IN Europe' (30 May 2016), the user condemned the Leave campaign for not knowing 'what happens after if we leave' (30 May 2016).

By contrast, seven out of eight key users in the core networks surrounding @Nigel_Farage were Pro-Brexit and passionate supporters of Farage. These users thanked Nigel Farage for promoting Brexit and praised him for saving democracy and bringing hopes to the UK. They spoke highly of Nigel Farage and what he had been advocating. Some of these key users even revealed that they had the UKIP membership. Their tweets contained six main themes (see Table 4.2).

The only one pro-Remain account: @StrongerInPress in Nigel Farage's core networks blamed him for ignoring the impact of Brexit on 'working families', tariffs, 'the single market', 'the economy' and 'sterling'. It also mocked Farage for not being knowledgeable and for failing to respond to questions appropriately.

Topic Modelling

The topics emerging from topic modelling of the 107,710 tweets mentioning @David_Cameron resonate with the findings from the social network analysis

Table 4.1. Themes in the Tweets Published by (Key) Leave Users in @David_Cameron's Core Networks.

Theme Numbers	Themes	Example Tweets (All Rephrased Except the First Tweet)
1	Self-declaring to be Brexiteers; calling to leave and take back control to 'restore democracy'	No @David_Cameron Britain doesn't quit. We are determined to restore democracy to this country #VoteLeave (by @Vote_LeaveMedia) (7 June 2016)
2	Labelling David Cameron as a traitor, liar and scaremonger	what a liar David Cameron is (22 June 2016)
3	The failure of David Cameron and the EU	@David_Cameron ultimately failed to reform the EU which could not be amended #InOrOut #VoteLeave (2 June 2016)
4	Poor media performances of David Cameron	@David_Cameron is tortured and destroyed on Friday #BBCdebate #IndependenceDay #VoteLeave (21 June 2016)
5	Only David Cameron and rich people wanted to remain	@David_Cameron Your policy is to let the rich have the benefits but let the poor suffer austerity. I do not believe you. I #voteleave! (17 June 2016)
6	David Cameron failed to keep immigration under control and lied about immigration	@David_Cameron is a liar: (he) knew he would not meet the immigration target four years ago (22 June 2016)
7	David Cameron helped Turkey join the EU	@David_Cameron @Conservatives You used our money to help Turkey join the EU rather than spending it on our NHS #VoteLeave (9 June 2016)

and thematic analysis of his core networks and the messages sent by the key users in these networks. There are three prominent themes in these topics (Table 4.3): (1) self-declaring their decision or action to vote leave (Topics 1–7), (2) supporting Remain and David Cameron (Topics 1, 3 and 7) and (3)

Table 4.2. Themes in the Tweets Published by (Key) Leave Users in @Nigel_Farage's Core Networks.

Theme Numbers	Themes	Example Tweets (All Rephrased)
1	Self-declaring to be Brexiteers (and even UKIP members) and calling to vote leave	Nigel, well done! @Nigel_Farage is a real patriot. I am proud to be a member of the UKIP. Thank you (10 June 2016)
2	Excellent performances of Farage in debates and his successful campaign	@Nigel_Farageon had outstanding performances and outperformed David Cameron. His responses were open and honest, while David Cameron and George Osborne were aggressive and thought themselves superior (to us) #VoteLeave (12 June 2016)
3	Farage speaks the truth and is a hero	@Nigel_Farage is a star. He always speaks the truth. This is how we can be free from the shackles of the EU #VoteLeave (10 June 2016)
4	Remainers want to give our country away	@Nigel_Farage Remainers want to give away this country that we built and to betray this nation, for which we fought and died. I am voting #Brexit (23 June 2016)
5	The benefits of Brexit	@Nigel_Farage YES, Brexit can make export cheaper #BREXIT (12 June 2016)
6	Blaming immigrants, immigration and Muslims	#Brexit #UKIP #VoteLeave @Nigel_Farage Muslims are a threat as shown in India, Leave #EU (6 June 2016)

accusing David Cameron, George Osborne and Remainers of lying (Topics 3, 4, 6 and 7). The weighting of each topic indicates that the second theme of supporting Remain and David Cameron is relatively weaker than the other two. By contrast, the other two themes and related topics are prominent and dominant. These two themes and topics suggest a strong expression of Leave

Table 4.3. Topics Emerging from LDA Topic Modelling of Tweets Mentioning @David_Cameron.

Topic Numbers	Labels	Indicating Words with Highest Values	Percentages of the Whole Corpus
1	Vote leave versus Vote remain	david_cameron, euref, brexit, strongerin, leave, remain, case, problem, want, basis, get, apart, UK, conservative, referendum, EU, well, stay, nigel_farage, debate, vote_leave, tonight, come, labour, immigration, look, BBC, euvoteleave, side, ITV	46.5%
2	Vote leave, immigration, and independence	voteleave, vote, bbcnews, say, know, British, right, day, June, wake, never, meanwhile, euro, tunnel, Calais, outside, win, louisemensch, MPs, agree, michaelcaine, say, answer, mean, big, ivote, independence, stitch, hope, small, business, ivotedleave, year	17.7%
3	Vote remain, vote leave, and lie	voteremain, even, stronger_together, lie, incredibly, passionate, Britain, today, tell, close, stop, strong, late, future, morning, poll, Samantha, see, secure, junckereu, Ireland, leaveeu, put, not, offer, leadership, resign, junker, risk, save, nation, new	9.5%
4	Vote leave, lie	Turn, make, true, people, speech, go, dave, thanks, need, prime, minister, Europe, way, job, letter, junckereu, peston, deal, brexitnoww, join, care, list, far, voteout, kid, tweet	8.9%

5	Take back control, vote leave, and David Cameron's rally at the University of Birmingham	Party, country, control, reform, Cameron, back, support, peston, tomorrow, talk, believe, democracy, endorsement, cunt, currently, campus, delighted, welcome, unibirmingham, world, happen, deliver, loose, sovereignty	6.8%
6	Take back control, vote leave, and liar politicians (in particular, David Cameron and George Osborne)	Tory, thing, think, george_osborne, sure, undecided, peston, imagine, pay, ponzi-scheme, trillion, euro, liarpoliticians, give, takebackcontrol, seem, use, paxman, ireland, regardless, public, fix, bigots_racist, fascists, moron, disgust, retweet, simonschama	5.8%
7	Leave, Remainers lied, supporting Remain and David Cameron	Lose, eureferendum, result, voter, time, promise, ukleave_eu, change, trust, keep, jamesberrymp, whatever, takecontrol, call, part, rich, bite, quit, many, peace, enough, benatipsosmori, independenceday, majority, European, union, find, exaggerate, false, econ, claim	4.8%

stance and of condemnation of David Cameron and his Remain arguments, alongside a relatively weak support expressed for Remain, in the tweets of users who mentioned @David_Cameron.

On the contrary, the seven topics (Table 4.4) identified in topic modelling of the 119,318 tweets that mentioned @Nigel_Farage only contain three types of themes about: (1) the determination and action to vote leave, which was seen to save British democracy (Topics 1, 4, and 5), (2) casting doubts on David Cameron and the Remain campaign (Topics 1 and 2) and (3) supporting Farage and the UKIP, taking back control (Britain first), and viewing Brexit as a hope and a measure to save British democracy (Topics 3, 4, 6 and 7). Themes 1 and 2 have some overlaps.

These themes and topics identified from LDA topic modelling are coherent with and supported by those from our qualitative analysis of related tweets containing indicating words of salience, such as 'voteleave', 'ivotedleave', 'stronerin', 'lie', 'liar', 'pencilgate', 'dodgy', 'annietrev' and 'racism'. 'Voteleave' and 'ivotedleave' appeared mostly as hashtags '#voteleave' and '#ivotedleave'. 'Voteleave' appeared more than 40,000 times, more than double the times 'strongerin' appearing in the corpus of the dataset. These tweets containing either or both of 'voteleave' and 'ivotedleave' largely expressed the users' decision or action of voting leave.

'Lie' and 'liar' were also salient terms appearing more than 5,000 times in the whole dataset. The tweets containing one or more of the words: 'lie, 'lies' or 'liar' portrayed David Cameron as a liar who kept telling lies. The term of 'dodgy' was frequently used to refer to David Cameron in the hashtag #DodgyDave or in the phrase 'Dodgy Dave', as exemplified in the tweet (Rephrased): It is Great Britain for @Nigel_Farage but Little England for #DodgyDave (7 June 2016). Sometimes the term of 'dodgy' also appeared in the tweets talking about 'dodgy leaflets' circulated by the Remain campaign, or referring to David Cameron's 'dodgy govt' (dodgy government). Taken together, the analysis points to that David Cameron was under siege and criticised by users who responded to him but supported Leave.

Likewise, the word 'pencilgate' was often included in the hashtag '#pencilgate' in the tweets in relation to Brexit supporters' scepticism over why pencils were used in polling stations. The term 'annietrev', which was the twitter handle of Anne-Marie Trevelyan who was in favour of Brexit, was used in a viral tweet. This tweet contains a short video showing that the staff in a polling station were doing things that looked like erasing and tampering votes written with pencils. The term of 'racism' was mostly used in the context where Nigel Farage (and the Leave campaign) was accused of 'legitimising racism', but his supporters strongly defended him and refuted this accusation in their tweets.

Table 4.4. Topics Emerging from LDA Topic Modelling of Tweets Mentioning @Nigel_Farage.

Topic No.	Label	Indicating Words with Highest Values	Percentage of the Whole Corpus
1	Voteleave, scepticism about the Remain campaign	nigel_farage, voteleave, Remain, dodgy, brexit, vote, leave, hope, take, control, let, border, pencilgate, go, leaveeu, uk, betteroffout, know, Britain, pollster, bookie, referendum, woman, vote_leave, everyone, make good, borisjohnson, fight, one	46.5%
2	Scepticism about the Remain campaign	Euref, look, ivote, annietrev, pencilgate	16.9%
3	UKIP, the war rhetoric	Skynews, do, UKIP, win, leader, war, battle, god, Euro-sceptic, genie, bottle, turkey, break, bring	9.9%
4	Vote leave and take back control	back, country, together, get, democracy, time, heard, labourleave	9.5%
5	Vote leave	ivotedleave, people, British, today, year, want, politician, Europe	8.4%
6	Britain first, praising Nigel Farage	bit, day, give, turn, think, work, voting, campaign, applause, hard, nation, britainfirst, place, salute, heart, soul, European, forever, London	6%
7	Making racist remarks, expressing accusations against Nigel Farage, defending Nigel Farage	Great, friend, racist, last, cheer, tomorrow, feistydeanne, ukipskipton, proxy, night, duty, fascist, fuck, emotional, sacrifice, foreign, body	2.8%

To summarise, the topic modelling and the qualitative analysis of the tweets mentioning either or both of @David_Cameron and @Nigel_Farage expose a stark contrast in how Twitter users viewed the two politicians. Overall, these tweets were largely hostile toward David Cameron, attacking him as a liar and loser. In the meantime, Nigel Farage was defended and hailed as a hero.

DISCUSSION AND CONCLUSION

This chapter aimed to understand whether, and to what extent, Twitter users approved or disapproved of David Cameron and Nigel Farage when they responded to the two politicians in their tweets. The findings suggest that Twitter users chose to side with one of them. In one politician's 'echo chamber', Twitter users presented strong disagreement with and disapproval of the other. Notably, Nigel Farage won much more 'like-minded' supporters than David Cameron did. In this sense, Twitter communication about the referendum wove robust supporting networks for Nigel Farage but formed a contentious space where David Cameron was ruthlessly attacked.

Therefore, the findings of this study partly echo those of existing studies discussed above, showing politically alike individuals are connected. The political homophily and 'echo chamber' effects were extremely noticeable in Leave users' favourable response to @Nigel_Farage. The tweets of these users provided a sturdy suppor for Nigel Farage, legitimising his Brexit stance and arguments and even the UKIP.

With that said, this research has presented a clear counter-argument: instead of holding shared views, users may approach politicians because of their political disagreement. It was evident that @David_Cameron was under siege in mostly oppositional networks. The majority of the tweets mentioning or retweeting @David_Cameron expressed disagreement with David Cameron and denounced him. Encountering the Remain stance and arguments of David Cameron, users did not reassess their positions, but sharply criticised him and even labelled him a 'liar' or 'scaremonger'. Their criticism and attacks on David Cameron demonstrated ideological confrontation, which delegitimised him and his Remain arguments. The analysis shows the role played by political disagreement and ideological confrontation in shaping social media discussion and participation.

In this case, therefore, ideological disagreement and confrontation were as much evident and overwhelming as users' shared political views and values were in shaping their tweeting practices – more specifically how they responded to the two politicians. Instead of following along party lines, the polarised political disagreement and antagonism between Remain and Leave supporters were cutting across political parties and deeply and intricately rooted in British society. Underlying the outcome of the referendum on the UK's membership was deep divisions in British society and politics (Goodwin & Heath, 2016; Kagarlitsky, 2017). The Brexit vote was the manifestation of the anger of those, who had been 'left behind' (Goodwin & Heath, 2016). In this 'populist referendum' (Iakhnis et al., 2018), the UKIP, which had been advocating withdrawing the UK from the EU since its launch in the late 1990s, underpinned the Leave campaign and the public support for Nigel Farage. Nigel Farage appeared to represent those who were 'the "left behind" – social groups that were united by a general sense of insecurity, pessimism and marginalisation' and that were anti-elitists (Goodwin & Heath, 2016, p. 331). By contrast, David Cameron was speaking in the voice of those elite members – who were believed to have benefited from the global and liberal world order and thus refused to change it. Such a deep and strong disagreement between the two groups was not negotiable, and it would be massively difficult to have a democratic dialogue between them. Thus, there was little room for a deliberative discussion.

In theory, with the technological affordances of Twitter, both Leave and Remain users were able to express disagreement with or support for the politicians. However, the differences in the social media practices of Leave and Remain users influenced the levels of expression of their political values. In the 'third space' on social media (Wright, Graham, & Jackson, 2016), the active participation of Leave users led to the formation of Leave voices, which were much 'louder' than those of Remain users. While Remain users did not actively form supportive networks for @David_Cameron, Leave users provided @Nigel_Farage with enormous support in tandem with their rampant attacks on @David_Cameron. On Twitter, @David_Cameron was surrounded, attacked and delegitimised by Leave users, who supported and saluted @Nigel_Farage as a hero and saviour instead. It is unclear whether such an attack was organised by the Leave Campaign, or it happened spontaneously among Leave users. It is, however, certain that Leave users had made more active use of the technological affordances of Twitter than Remain users did.

The study reported in this chapter suggests a potential connection between social media sentiment and actual public opinion. The antagonism held by Leave users toward David Cameron indicates that there were a group of people who were angry about and intolerant of the status quo of the UK's EU membership before the referendum. In addition, the findings draw our attention to the role played by the Leave campaign, in particular Nigel Farage and the UKIP, in the run-up to the referendum. This leads to the question of whether, and to what extent, the blatant attacks on David Cameron were actually organised and manipulated by the Leave campaign. Early monitoring of social media messages and networks would help political campaigning as well as detect political manipulation. More research, in particular, which involves empirical research with Twitter users and key figures from the Leave campaign, would be helpful.

5

SHAPING POLITICAL DISCOURSE: IS TWITTER GOOD FOR DEMOCRACY?

This concluding chapter will discuss how Twitter worked in shaping political discourse about the referendum and what implications this case has for understanding the democratic potential of Twitter and the problems of political communication in the social media era. In Western democratic societies, while the news media succumb to commercial and political influences, they have become dysfunctional in terms of playing their expected role in democracy. Hope has been given to the Internet to function as an alternative medium for facilitating political communication that a healthy democracy needs. Nevertheless, this study reported in this book casts doubts on the contribution that the Internet in general, and in particular Twitter, can make to democracy.

In this case, the dual role played by Twitter as a space for articulating polarised public opinion and for spreading populism reveals the mechanisms of Twitter for shaping political discourse. Crucial to its dual role were the everyday experiences, tweeting skills and strategies of users as well as political disagreement among them. Although being a crucial part of political communication, Twitter communication showed a dangerous potential for aggravating political disagreement between Leave and Remain supporters and for mainstreaming and boosting populism. This perilous potential deteriorated – rather than mitigated or helped to fix – the long-existing problems in political communication, such as the inability of the news media to explain the complexity of political issues. The hope that social media can serve democracy well is, thus, dim. Twitter communication appeared to be a double-edged sword. At the same time of enabling public participation and engagement of users, Twitter communication, however, posed a risk of exacerbating tensions and divisions in society, oversimplifying the complexity of social issues, and being influenced or even being manipulated by individuals and social groups to serve their own private interests.

TWITTER'S DUAL ROLE AND POLITICAL DISCOURSE OF THE BREXIT REFERENDUM

This study reveals two roles played by Twitter in influencing the political discourse of the Brexit referendum. First, Twitter became a platform for users to voice their understandings of the UK-EU relationship and the UK's EU membership. This role demonstrates Twitter's potential to function as a weather vane of public sentiment. Public opinion on Twitter about the referendum, however, was primarily split between imagining the EU membership as a necessary blessing and seeing it as a disaster. This divide mirrors the opposition between pro-globalisation, pro-European integration political values and those supporting populism. Users' responses to David Cameron and Nigel Farage also reflected the ideological confrontation between the two sides of the debate about the referendum.

Second, Twitter provided a fertile space for populism to grow in and to be mainstreamed in the month leading up to the Brexit referendum. In addition to the overall prominent expression of populist ideas on Twitter, the tweets of key British politicians and news media legitimised and mainstreamed populism into the debate about the referendum. Meanwhile, Nigel Farage and his populist views were embraced and praised widely by Leave supporters. By contrast, David Cameron mostly received verbal abuse and hostility from Leave users and was delegitimised and denounced by them. Populist politicians, in particular Nigel Farage, gained considerable influence through users' tweeting practices. As a result of the dual role, Twitter communication about the referendum constructed a political discourse of contention and confrontation – in particular, against pro-European integration – and that of populism.

Instead of purely benefiting from its decentralised technical structure, Twitter gains its capacity to play the dual role from the tweeting practices of users. The importance of users' practices was partly shown in tweeting as an everyday practice. Users' understandings of the EU membership were expressed through the association of the membership with everyday concepts and objects. The importance of the tweeting practices of users was also demonstrated in the communication style and tactics as well as interactions of users – not only politicians and the news media but also ordinary users, in particular, Leave users – leading to the expression, spread and legitimation of populism on Twitter.

THE DEMOCRATIC POTENTIAL OF TWITTER COMMUNICATION

Twitter communication should be understood as part of the broader mediated political communication processes. On the one hand, it would be inappropriate to claim that political communication is transformed entirely under the sway of Twitter communication, or to argue that Twitter has a paramount influence on public opinion. It would also be difficult to determine 'quantitatively' how much impact Twitter communication has had on politics – specifically, the outcome of the referendum in this case. In addition, Twitter cannot represent social media, as user behaviours differ across social media platforms (Valenzuela, Correa, & Zúñiga, 2018).

On the other hand, however, Twitter communication is an important supplement to media communication. While the traditional news media have been criticised for being disconnected from local communities and for losing public trust, social media platforms like Twitter are needed to provide an alternative space for ordinary users to express their concerns, views and even emotions. However, it is uncertain to what extent social media like Twitter can contribute to the wellbeing of democracy and can help fix the existing problems of political communication.

The Ills of Political Communication

In the context of the UK, maintaining a healthy democracy requires the news media to provide 'a full and effective representation of citizens' political views and interests' to ensure media pluralism, so that voters can access different values and vote 'correctly' in elections or referenda (Dunleavy & Taylor, 2017, p. 70). The media system in Britain helps achieve the goal of media pluralism. While the BBC and other broadcasters are expected to remain neutral and impartial, the UK press have their own partisan orientations and advocate their preferred values to mobilise readers.

However, the British news media have been criticised for failing these ideals generally, and, in particular, during the referendum campaign (Payne, 2018; Seaton, 2016). With the decade-long withering of local journalism in the UK, local communities were thought to no longer be properly represented and heard in local or national media outlets. Their lack of representation in media coverage and the feeling of being disconnected from the news media had with distrust of led to local communities' growing hostility toward the news media (Seaton, 2016). Most UK news coverage of Brexit reflected the divisive nature of the Brexit topic but contained insufficient information to explain its complexity. What worsened the situation was that even when multiple views were voiced in the media coverage of the referendum, the public might simply avoid reading or stop believing them (Payne, 2018). The inability of the traditional news media to provide media pluralism and to engage audiences was also thought to be partly responsible for the significant polarisation in the online world in general and in particular, in relation to the Brexit referendum (Seaton, 2016).

Before the arrival of social media, the mainstream news media set and interpreted agendas for the public, drawing their attention to important issues and shaping public opinion on these issues (McCombs & Shaw, 1972). Although the public had – and still have – the freedom to choose whatever values that looked appealing to them, the political values of news outlets often matched those of their readers. The opinions of these news outlets, resonating with their readers, could be powerful and influential during political events. As a result, the political ideas and values promoted by the press often swayed public opinion. For example, with a vast readership, *The Sun* was criticised for manipulating public opinion and British politics in favour of the political parties it backed in the UK general elections of 1992 and 1997 (McNair, 2004).

In the wake of the popularity of social media, the mainstream news media have encountered difficulties in influencing public opinion. With the arrival of social media, the news media have lost their monopoly over information production and dissemination. They have to compete with other media platforms such as blogs, YouTube and Twitter for agenda-setting power (Meraz, 2009; Sayre, Bode, Shah, Wilcox, & Shah, 2010). Discourses constructed on social media can also influence the public's interpretation of related social issues. Using social media, elite members, such as politicians, can approach the public directly without needing the mediation of the news media. They may even overtake the news media to become 'new' agenda-setters in the online sphere of social media, weakening the agenda-setting role and power of the news media. Additionally, the attacks on journalism by politicians like Donald Trump would further damage the credibility and cultural authority of the news media that have already started losing audience engagement.[1]

1 Since being elected as the president of the United States, Donald Trump had kept aggressively attacking journalism and the news media, such as the *New York Times*, and labelled them as producing 'fake news' and practising 'bad journalism'. His hostility and attacks erode public trust in journalism and deteriorated the legitimacy of journalism (Lischka, 2019).

The Promises and Problems of Social Media Communication (As Shown in This Case)

On social media platforms like Twitter, which provide users with an alternative, unmediated front stage of communication (Wodak, 2009), those, who are disappointed with and have lost trust in the mainstream news media, are able to speak out their voices. In this regard, social media has democratic potential for enabling the exchange of information and opinions on an unprecedented scale and for diversifying agendas in the public sphere. However, it is uncertain to what extent we can fully achieve this democratic potential. Although potentially increasing the level of plurality in opinions, ordinary users' access to online communication means that information and content that are published by them are not bound by journalism professional standards and principles of practice. They may be biased, sensational, emotional and lacking accuracy, and thus may not do democracy any good.

As revealed in this case, the polarised views in Twitter communication oversimplified and reduced the complexity of the Brexit issue to the simplicity of being 'black and white' (a term of Jean Seaton, 2016). Additionally, stirred up by populist politicians and Leave users, public sentiments in support of populism were prominent on Twitter. Twitter communication about the referendum was hijacked by those holding populist views, fuelling the spread of populism and helping populist politicians gain political influence. These problems, thus, draw our attention to the mutual impact between social media communication and social and political dynamics and change.

As discussed earlier in the book, the Brexit vote emerged in a context of social divisions and rising populism. In Western democratic societies like the UK, the US, France, Italy and Poland, the contest of political values has led to divided public opinion and unexpected election results that signal the winning of national populism. Nationalist populism has arisen as an alternative political ideology which stresses the necessity to protect the national interest and the interests of locals. It is the opposite of the dominant political ideologies that embrace globalisation and global liberal capitalism and that have prevailed since the 1990s. There have been academic efforts to examine the relationship between populism and public communication (see, for example, articles in Aalberg, Esser, Reinemann, Strömback, & de Vreese, 2017) in general, and social media in particular, which has been thought to facilitate the rise of nationalist populism (Gerbaudo, 2018). This study shares the worries of scholars about the role played by social media in fuelling the spread of populism and enabling populist politicians to distribute their populist claims and to mobilise and enlist supporters (Blassnig et al., 2020; Engesser, Ernst,

Esser, & Büchel, 2017; Ernst, Engesser, Büchel, Blassnig, & Esser, 2017; Groshek & Engelbert, 2013; Reinemann, Aalberg, Esser, Strömbäck, & de Vreese, 2017; Stier, Posch, Bleier, & Strohmaier., 2017).

Populism spreads through multiple channels. In the British context, right-wing news outlets such as *The Daily Telegraph* and *The Sun* have been facilitating the discussion of populism with their constant focus on issues like immigration. Politicians, adopting diverse strategies, were blamed for spreading populism on social media, and they, thus, were responsible for the spread of this fragmented ideology (Engesser et al., 2017). Right-wing politicians like Nigel Farage have actively used not only the mainstream media but also social media to promulgate their populist ideas among supporters. Diverse factors – including the popularity and pervasiveness of social media, the waiving of the gate-keeping of the news media, and the absence of adherence to professional principles, as well as the accessible styles and social media tactics of populist politicians – make it easy for populist discourses to blossom on social platforms.

Nevertheless, it would be wrong to assume social media functions as a mirror that accurately reflects the opinions of every single man and woman. Many other factors in reality, such as access to social media, available resources at the disposal of users and the levels of their digital literacy, would restrict users from speaking out on social media. In addition, in theory, while there are contesting values, social media would not convey merely one type of political values. In practice, however, only those who proactively and strategically use social media are able to make their voices heard on social media. This study, for example, demonstrates that although social media created opportunities for both Leave and Remain users to promote their arguments, the 'voices' of Brexit users, who were more actively promoting their views, were 'louder' than those of Remain users. Likewise, when it comes to politicians, populist politicians like Nigel Farage who well used Twitter to promulgate their populist claims gained more influence and prominence than Remain politicians. Remain politicians were active but appeared to have misunderstood the mechanisms of user interactions on Twitter. In this case, thus, it was the tweeting practices of users that led to the articulation and legitimation of populism on Twitter.

The legitimising and mainstreaming of populism were the result of four factors, as revealed in this study: (1) the social media strategies and practices of populist politicians and their political mobilisation, (2) the tweeting practices of the news media under the influence of their journalistic practices and the word limit of Twitter, (3) the tweeting practices of Remain politicians who appeared to have misunderstood how Twitter works, (4) the sticking together and aggressive attacks of Leave users on Remain politicians and on their pro-globalisation and pro-EU claims – although it is unclear whether the Leave political campaign organised this or it was merely naturally occurring among users. The 'echo chamber' effect led to a situation where 'like-minded' users adhered together to form online communities, reinforcing their opinions and speaking out collective, 'clamorous' voices of populism. In this case, the campaign strategies and tweeting practices of populist politicians and Leave users gave rise to the prominence of populist politicians, provided justification for their claims, but, meanwhile, delegitimised pro-EU politicians and their arguments. A contentious and confrontational sphere on Twitter was thus formed, where complex issues surrounding the Brexit referendum may be oversimplified and democracy may not be served well.

It remains unclear whether, and to what extent, the expression of polarised public sentiments and the articulation and legitimation of populism in Twitter communication influenced the Brexit vote. As discussed above, Twitter is merely one medium of communication, alongside the mainstream news media and other social media platforms such as Facebook and Instagram. The findings of this study, therefore, cannot be generalised to all kinds of social media communication.

However, one sure thing is that neither political polarisation nor the prevailing of populism will help the wellbeing of democracy. Although populism may act as a political correction to democracy (Kaltwasser, 2012), and its merits of populism to democracy are open to debate, the populist threat to liberal democracy has been widely recognised (see, for example, Galston, 2018; Mounk, 2014; Painter, 2013; Weyland, 2013). Therefore, despite the Brexit referendum and social media gave a much-needed boost to political engagement in the UK (Hall, Tinati, & Jennings, 2018; Payne, 2018), such political engagement may not do democracy a favour nor fix the existing problems of political communication.

THE PRECARIOUS FUTURE OF POLITICAL COMMUNICATION IN THE SOCIAL MEDIA ERA

What is clearly emerging from this study is the perilous potential of social media to reflect and reinforce social tensions and divisions and to be influenced or even manipulated by individuals or social groups to serve their own interests. We are living in a time when Donald Trump, the US president at the time of writing (in 2019 and 2020), tweeted 'when looting starts, shooting starts' to incite violence in response to the nationwide protests over the murder of George Floyd. This is also a time when terrorists live-streamed their indiscriminate killing of innocent civilians (Flynn, 2019; Klonick, 2019). In such a time, identifying and understanding the potential danger of social media is particularly essential for fostering healthy political communication. That social media communication can go wrong would make the already bad situation in relation to political communication worse. While a regulatory intervention may be needed to police social media content – a full discussion of this issue is beyond the scope of this book, the news media need to continue to shoulder the responsibility of informing and setting agendas for the public for the sake of democracy.

Over the last few years, the world has witnessed political uncertainty, turbulence and volatility, to which the disruptive Brexit drama has contributed. Rampant, deadly terror attacks killed civilians in countries like the UK, the United States (US), France, Australia and New Zealand.[2,3,4,5,6] The COVID-19 health and political crises and the Black Lives Matter protests swamped the world in 2020.[7,8] The long-term tensions between the US and China were exacerbated by events such as their escalated trade war, the US sanctions on Huawei, a Chinese technology company, Donald Trump and his supporters pointing fingers at China during the coronavirus pandemic, and the forced closure of Houston and Chengdu Consulates.[9,10] These tumultuous

2 See, for example, https://news.sky.com/story/terror-in-the-uk-timeline-of-attacks-11833061 (Accessed on July 6, 2020).

3 See, for example, https://edition.cnn.com/2013/04/18/us/u-s-terrorist-attacks-fast-facts/index.html (Accessed on July 6, 2020).

4 See, for example, https://www.ft.com/content/22db9a76-de30-42ff-a155-56594a3dbdfb and https://www.cbsnews.com/paris-attacks/ (Accessed on July 6, 2020).

5 See, for example, https://time.com/5075253/terrorist-attacks-australia-timeline/ (Accessed on July 6, 2020).

6 See, for example, https://www.independent.co.uk/topic/new-zealand-attack (Accessed on July 6, 2020).

7 Although the coronavirus pandemic is a health crisis, it also poses a threat to the legitimacy of governments and politicians over their handling of the outbreak.

8 The Black Lives Matter movement was triggered by the death of George Floyd who was killed in police enforcement over a suspected fake $20 note in the United States in 2020. This anti-racism movement engulfed the American society and spread to regions and countries like Canada, Europe, the UK and Australia.

9 See, for example, https://www.bbc.co.uk/news/business-45899310 (Accessed on July 6, 2020).

10 See, for example, https://www.theguardian.com/us-news/2020/jul/22/china-us-ordered-abrupt-closure-houston-consulate-texas and https://www.thetimes.co.uk/article/chinese-consulate-staff-in-houston-tried-to-steal-scientific-secrets-35x2nrbrb (Accessed on July 31, 2020).

events have brought to the fore important issues – such as terrorism, racism, populism, nationalism, national security and social inequalities – societies across the world face and need to address. In such turbulent times, while we allow the political meanings of these events to unfold, it is particularly important to understand what role social media play in addressing related issues, tensions, changes and uncertainty in society and politics.

This study contends that it is necessary to be aware of social media's potential to aggravate social tensions and divisions and to be manipulated by certain social groups or individuals. During politically volatile times, social media communication may exacerbate social tensions, uncertainty and contention, rather than rationally explaining contextual reasons and therefore helping alleviate these tensions. Some political opportunists such as Donald Trump may even seek to manipulate social media to mobilise and enlist supporters to serve their own particular interests. Therefore, hoping social media to come to the rescue of democracy by acting as an alternative space for users may end in vain.

This study resonates with the growing scepticism over the capacity of social media communication to facilitate healthy political discussions (see, for example, Jaidka, Zhou, & Lelkes, 2020; Keller, Schoch, Stier, & Yang, 2020). Over recent years, apart from the widespread concerns over hate speech online (Gelashvili, 2018), attention has been paid to the increasing problems of misinformation, disinformation and political manipulation (Badawy, Ferrara, & Lerman, 2018; Broniatowski et al., 2018; Keller et al., 2020; Linvill & Warren, 2020; Margolin, Hannak, & Weber, 2018). These concerns point to the importance of figuring out a way to strike a balance between policing social media content and maintaining freedom of expression on social media, the topic of which deserves more profound discussions in future research.

As the research reported in this book shows, ordinary users, the news media, politicians and political parties have to understand how social media works in influencing political discourse if they want to use social media to strengthen or reinvigorate democracy. However, it would not be enough to only rely on individual users to increase their social media literacy or to behave in a way that is beneficial to democracy. While preserving the freedom of expression on social media is crucial for democracy, healthy political communication would also require to monitor and moderate social media content. These measures are aimed to ensure that the freedom of expression on social media will not be abused and exploited by individuals and interest groups to serve their private interests but undermine the public interest. Early monitoring of social media content can help detect public sentiments and manipulation of public opinion in social media communication. High levels of antagonism expressed on social media may reduce complex social issues to the expression of sheer anger and even hatred toward those holding opposite values and beliefs. Content moderation – a practice involving the use of computer tools such as artificial intelligence (AI) and human moderators to filter or remove content that is harmful, hateful or inaccurate – may contribute to reducing the levels of antagonism on social media. In the meantime, of course, social media content monitoring and moderation should not be used to exercise censorship.

In addition to the need to monitor and moderate social media communication, the news media should continue to play an important – or even more important than ever – role in fostering a healthy public sphere. While the problems of social media communication are gradually exposed, the news media must solve their long-lasting issues so that they can better serve communities and democracy. However, it is precarious whether, and to what extent, the news media can regain public trust and win the battle against the influence of social media on public opinion. Therefore, the study reported in this book raises an alarm: in the social media era, political communication is in danger, and much needs to be done to find solutions to this predicament.

REFERENCES

Aalberg, T., Esser, F., Reinemann, C., Strömback, J., & de Vreese, C. (Eds.), (2017). *Populist political communication in Europe*. London: Routledge.

Agarwal, A., Singh, R., & Toshniwal, D. (2018). Geospatial sentiment analysis using Twitter data for UK-EU referendum. *Journal of Information and Optimization Sciences*, *39*(1), 303–317.

Akkerman, T., Lange, S. L. d., & Rooduijn, M. (Eds.), (2016). *Radical Right-Wing populist parties in Western Europe: Into the mainstream?* Oxon; New York, NY: Routledge.

Al-garadi, M. A., Varathan, K. D., & Ravana, S. D. (2016). Cybercrime detection in online communications: The experimental case of cyberbullying detection in the Twitter network. *Computers in Human Behavior*, *63*, 433–443.

Almond, G. A., & Verba, S. (1963). *The civic culture: Political attitudes and democracy in five nations*. Princeton, NJ: Princeton University Press.

Alvares, C., & Dahlgren, P. (2016). Populism, extremism and media: Mapping an uncertain terrain. *European Journal of Communication*, *31*(1), 46–57.

Ang, I. (1991). *Living room wars: Rethinking media audiences for a postmodern world*. New York, NY; London: Routledge.

Anstead, N., & O'Loughlin, B. (2015). Social media analysis and public opinion: The 2010 UK General Election. *Journal of Computer-Mediated Communication*, *20*(2), 204–220.

Antony, M. G., & Thomas, R. J. (2010). 'This is citizen journalism at its finest': YouTube and the public sphere in the Oscar Grant shooting incident. *New Media & Society*, *12*(8), 1280–1296.

Arda, B. (2015). The construction of a new sociality through social media: The case of the Gezi uprising in Turkey. *Conjunctions. Transdisciplinary Journal of Cultural Participation*, *2*(1), 72–99.

Badawy, A., Ferrara, E., & Lerman, K. (2018). Analyzing the digital traces of political manipulation: The 2016 Russian interference Twitter campaign. Paper presented at the IEEE/ACM International Conference on Advances in Social Networks Analysis and Mining (ASONAM).

Bakshy, E., Messing, S., & Adamic, L. A. (2015). Exposure to ideologically diverse news and opinion on Facebook. *Science*, *5*, 1130–1132. doi:10.1126/science.aaa1160.

Barberá, P., Jost, J. T., Nagler, J., Tucker, J. A., & Bonneau, R. (2015). Tweeting from left to right: Is online political communication more than an echo chamber? *Psychological Science*, *26*(10), 1531–1542.

Barnard, S. R. (2012). Twitter and the journalistic field: How the Growth of a new(s) Medium is transforming journalism. *PhD*. The University of Missouri, Missouri.

Bastos, M. T., & Mercea, D. (2019). The Brexit Botnet and user-generated hyperpartisan news. *Social Science Computer Review*, *37*(1), 38–54.

Baviera, T., Peris, À., & Cano-Orón, L. (2019). Political candidates in infotainment programmes and their emotional effects on Twitter: An analysis of the 2015 Spanish general elections pre-campaign season. *Contemporary Social Science*, *14*(1), 144–156.

Bekafigo, M. A., & McBride, A. (2013). Who tweets about politics? Political participation of Twitter users during the 2011 gubernatorial elections. *Social Science Computer Review*, *31*(5), 625–643.

Birenbaum, G., & Villa, M. (2003). The media and neo-populism in France. In G. Mazzoleni, J. Stewart, & B. Horsfield (Eds.), *The media and neo-populism: A contemporary comparative analysis* (pp. 45–67). Westport: Praeger Publishers.

Blassnig, S., Ernst, N., Engesser, S., Esser, F., Davis, R., & Taras, D. (2020). Populism and social media popularity: How populist communication benefits political leaders on Facebook and Twitter. In D. Taras & R. Davis (Eds.), *Power shift? Political leadership and social media* (pp. 97–111). New York, NY; Oxon: Routledge.

Blei, D. M., Ng, A. Y., & Jordan, M. I. (2003). Latent Dirichlet allocation. *Journal of Machine Learning Research*, 993–1022.

Block, E., & Negrine, R. (2017). The populist communication style: Toward a critical framework. *International Journal of Communication*, *11*(20), 178–197.

Bode, L., & Dalrymple, K. E. (2016). Politics in 140 characters or less: Campaign communication, network interaction, and political participation on Twitter. *Journal of Political Marketing*, *15*(4), 311–332.

Bogen, K. W., Millman, C., Huntington, F., & Orchowski, L. M. (2018). A qualitative analysis of disclosing sexual victimization by# NotOkay during the 2016 presidential election. *Violence and Gender*, *5*(3), 174–181.

Bonacchi, C., Altaweel, M., & Krzyzanska, M. (2018). The heritage of Brexit: Roles of the past in the construction of political identities through social media. *Journal of Social Archaeology*, *18*(2), 174–192.

Bonikowski, B. (2016). Three lessons of contemporary populism in Europe and the United States. *Brown Journal of World Affairs*, *23*(9), 9–24.

Bonikowski, B. (2017). Ethno-nationalist populism and the mobilization of collective resentment. *The British Journal of Sociology*, *68*(S1), S181–S213. doi:10.1111/1468-4446.12325

Boomgaarden, H. G., Schuck, A. R. T., Elenbaas, M., & Vreese, C. H. d. (2011). Mapping EU attitudes: Conceptual and empirical dimensions of Euroscepticism and EU support. *European Union Politics*, *12*(2), 241–266.

Bossetta, M., Segesten, A. D., & Trenz, H.-J. (2018). Political participation on Facebook during Brexit: Does user engagement on media pages stimulate engagement with campaigns?. *Journal of Language and Politics*, *17*(2), 173–194.

Boutyline, A., & Willer, R. (2017). The social structure of political echo chambers: Variation in ideological homophily in online network. *Political Psychology*, *38*(3), 551–569.

Bracciale, R., & Martella, A. (2017). Define the populist political communication style: The case of Italian political leaders on Twitter. *Information, Communication & Society*, *20*(9), 1310–1329.

Braun, V., & Clarke, V. (2006). Using thematic analysis in psychology. *Qualitative Research in Psychology*, *3*(2), 77–101.

Brena, G., Brambilla, M., Ceri, S., Giovanni, M. D., Pierri, F., & Ramponi, G. (2019). News sharing user behaviour on Twitter: A comprehensive data collection of news articles and social interactions. Paper presented at the Proceedings of the International AAAI Conference on Web and Social Media.

Bright, J. (2018). Explaining the emergence of echo chambers on social media: the role of ideology and extremism. *Journal of Computer-Mediated Communication*, *23*(1), 17–33.

Broniatowski, D. A., Jamison, A. M., Qi, S., Alkulaib, L., Chen, T., Benton, A., . . . Dredze, M. (2018). Weaponized health communication: Twitter bots and Russian trolls amplify the vaccine debate. *American journal of public health*, *108*(10), 1378–1384.

Bruns, A., & Highfield, T. (2013). Political networks on Twitter: Tweeting the queensland state election. *Information, Communication & Society*, *16*(5), 667–691.

Ceron, A., Curini, L., Iacus, S. M., & Porro, G. (2014). Every tweet counts? How sentiment analysis of social media can improve our knowledge of citizens' political preferences with an application to Italy and France. *New Media & Society*, *16*(2), 340–358.

Coesemans, R., & Cock, B. D. (2017). Self-reference by politicians on Twitter: Strategies to adapt to 140 characters. *Journal of Pragmatics*. *116*, 37–50.

Colleoni, E., Rozza, A., & Arvidsson, A. (2014). Echo chamber or public sphere? Predicting political orientation and measuring political homophily in Twitter using big data. *Journal of Communication*, *64*(2), 317–332.

Corbett, S. (2016). The social consequences of Brexit for the UK and Europe: Euroscepticism, populism, Nationalism, and societal division. *International Journal of Social Quality*, *6*(1), 11–31.

Cox, J. B. (2013). Twitter, Facebook, blogs, and media-sharing sites in the classroom. In K. Langmia, T. C. M. Tyree, P. O'Brien, & I. Sturgis (Eds.), *Social media: Pedagogy and practice* (pp. 21–42). Lanham, MD; Plymouth: Library of Congress Control.

Cox, M. (2017). The rise of populism and the crisis of globalisation: Brexit, Trump and beyond. *Irish Studies in International Affairs*, *28*, 9–17.

Cuperus, R. (2007). *Populism against globalisation: A new European revolt rethinking immigration and integration: A new centre left agenda* (pp. 147–165) London: Policy Network.

Curran, G. (2004). Mainstreaming populist discourse: The race-conscious legacy of neo-populist parties in Australia and Italy. *Patterns of Prejudice*, *38*(1), 37–55. doi:10.1080/0031322032000185578

Dang-Xuan, L., Stieglitz, S., Wladarsch, J., & Neuberger, C. (2013). An investigation of influentials and the role of sentiment in political communication on Twitter during election periods. *Information, Communication & Society*, *16*(5), 795–825.

Deacon, D., & Wring, D. (2016). The UK Independence Party, populism and the British news media: Competition, collaboration or containment? *European Journal of Communication*, *31*(2), 169–184.

Del Vicario, M., Zollo, F., Caldarelli, G., Scala, A., & Quattrociocchi, W. (2017). Mapping social dynamics on Facebook: The Brexit debate. *Social Networks*, *50*, 6–16.

Dubois, E., & Blank, G. (2018). The echo chamber is overstated: The moderating effect of political interest and diverse media. *Information, Communication & Society*, *21*(5), 729–745. doi:10.1080/1369118X.2018.1428656

Dunleavy, P., & Taylor, R. (2017). The 2017 audit of UK democracy. Democratic Audit.

Eichenberg, R. C., & Dalton, R. J. (1993). Europeans and the European community: The dynamics of public support for European integration. *International Organization*, *47*(4), 507–534.

Ekström, M., Patrona, M., & Thornborrow, J. (2018). Right-wing populism and the dynamics of style: A discourse-analytic perspective on mediated political performances. *Palgrave Communications*, *4*(1), 1–11.

Ellison, N., & Hardey, M. (2013). Developing political conversations? Social media and English local authorities. *Information, Communication & Society*, *16*(6), 878–898.

Elmer, G. (2013). Live research: Twittering an election debate. *New Media & Society*, *15*(1), 18–30. doi:10.1177/1461444812457328

Engesser, S., Ernst, N., Esser, F., & Büchel, F. (2017). Populism and social media: How politicians spread a fragmented ideology. *Information, Communication & Society*, *20*(8), 1109–1126.

Enli, G. S., & Skogerbø, E. (2013). Personalised campaigns in party-centred politics: Twitter and Facebook as arenas for political communication. *Information, Communication & Society*, *16*(5), 757–774.

Ernst, N., Engesser, S., Büchel, F., Blassnig, S., & Esser, F. (2017). Extreme parties and populism: An analysis of Facebook and Twitter across six countries. *Information, Communication & Society*, *20*(9), 1347–1364.

Evans, M. S. (2014). A computational approach to qualitative analysis in large textual datasets. *PLOS One*, 9(2)e87908.

Evans, H., & Evans, H. (2016). Do women only talk about "female issues"? Gender and issue discussion on Twitter. *Online Information Review*, *40*(5), 660–672.

Evolvi, G. (2019). # Islamexit: Inter-group antagonism on Twitter. *Information, Communication & Society*, 22(3), 386–401.

Fanoulis, E., & Guerra, S. (2017). Anger and protest: Referenda and opposition to the EU in Greece and the United Kingdom. *Cambridge Review of International Affairs*, *30*(4), 305–324. doi:10.1080/09557571.2018.1431766

Festinger, L. (1954). A theory of social comparison processes. *Human Relations*, 7(2), 117–140.

Festinger, L. (1957). *A theory of cognitive dissonance*. Stanford, CA: Stanford University Press.

Figenschou, T. U., & Beyer, A. (2014). The limits of the debate: How the Oslo terror shook the Norwegian immigration debate. *The International Journal of Press/Politics*, *19*(4), 430–452.

Figenschou, T. U., & Ihlebæk, K. A. (2019). Challenging journalistic authority. *Journalism Studies*, *20*(9), 1221–1237. doi:10.1080/1461670X.2018.150086

Figenschou, T. U., & Thorbjørnsrud, K. (2017). Disruptive media events: Managing mediated dissent in the aftermath of terror. *Jouranalism Practice*, *11*(8), 942–959.

Flaxman, S. R., Goel, S., & Rao, J. M. (2013). Ideological segregation and the Effects of social media on news consumption SSRN 2363701. Retrieved from https://pdfs.semanticscholar.org/768e/b9576a9a478c95e8ed3434ea4752c4098aa7.pdf

Flynn, M. (2019, March 19th, 2019). No one who watched New Zealand shooter's video live reported it to Facebook, company says. *The Washington Post*. Retrieved from https://www.washingtonpost.com/nation/2019/03/19/

new-zealand-mosque-shooters-facebook-live-stream-was-viewed-thousands-times-before-being-removed/

Flyvbjerg, B. (2001). *Making social science matter: Why social science inquiry has failed and how it can succeed again.* Cambridge: Cambridge University Press.

Ford, R., & Goodwin, M. (2017). Britain after Brexit: A nation divided. *Journal of Democracy*, *28*(1), 17–30.

Franch, F. (2013). (Wisdom of the crowds) 2: 2010 UK election prediction with social media. *Journal of Information Technology & Politics*, *10*(1), 57–71. doi:10.1080/19331681.2012.705080

Freeden, M. (2017). After the Brexit referendum: Revisiting populism as an ideology. *Journal of Political Ideologies*, *22*(1), 1–11.

Galston, W. A. (2018). *Anti-pluralism: The populist threat to liberal democracy.* New Haven, CT; London: Yale University Press.

Garrett, R. K. (2009a). Echo chambers online?: Politically motivated selective exposure among Internet news users. *Journal of Computer-Mediated Communication*, *14*, 265–285. doi:10.1111/j.1083-6101.2009.01440.x

Garrett, R. K. (2009b). Politically motivated reinforcement seeking: Reframing the selective exposure debate. *Journal of Communication*, *59*, 676–699.

Gelashvili, T. (2018). Hate speech on social media: Implications of private regulation and governance gaps. Lund University, Lund. Retrieved from http://lup.lub.lu.se/luur/download?func=downloadFile&recordOId=8952399&fileOId=8952403

Gerbaudo, P. (2014). Populism 2.0: Social media activism, the generic Internet user and interactive direct democracy. In D. Trottier & C. Fuchs (Eds.), *Social media, politics and the state* (pp. 79–99). London; New York, NY: Routledge.

Gerbaudo, P. (2018). Social media and populism: An elective affinity? *Media, Culture & Society*, *40*(5), 745–753. doi:10.1177/0163443718772192

Gerber, E. R., Henry, A. D., & Lubell, M. (2013). Political homophily and collaboration in regional planning networks. *American Journal of Political Science*, *57*(3), 598–610.

Gilbert, E., Bergstrom, T., & Karahalios, K. (2009). Blogs are echo chambers: Blogs are echo chambers. Paper presented at the 2009 42nd Hawaii International Conference on System Sciences, Hawaii.

Golbeck, J., Grimes, J. M., & Rogers, A. (2010). Twitter use by the U.S. Congress. *Journal of the American Society for Information Science and Technology*, *61*(8), 1612–1621.

Goldie, D., Linick, M., Jabbar, H., & Lubienski, C. (2014). Using bibliometric and social media analyses to explore the "echo chamber" hypothesis. *Educational Policy*, *28*(2), 281–305.

Gonzalez-Polledo, E. (2016). Chronic media worlds: Social media and the problem of pain communication on Tumblr. *Social Media+ Society*, *2*(1). doi: 10.1177/2056305116628887

Goodwin, M. J., & Heath, O. (2016). The 2016 referendum, Brexit and the left behind: An aggregate-level analysis of the result. *The Political Quarterly*, *87*(3), 323–332.

Gorodnichenko, Y., Pham, T., & Talavera, O. (2018). Social media, sentiment and public opinions: Evidence from #Brexit and #USElection. National Bureau of Economic Research. Retrieved from https://rahwebdav.swan.ac.uk/repec/pdf/wp2018-01.pdf

Graham, T., Broersma, M., Hazelhoff, K., & Haar, G. v. t. (2013). Between broadcasting political messages and interacting with voters: The use of Twitter during the 2010 UK General Election campaign. *Information, Communication & Society*, *16*(5), 692–716.

Graham, T., Jackson, D., & Broersma, M. (2016). New platform, old habits? Candidates' use of Twitter during the 2010 British and Dutch general election campaigns. *New Media & Society*, *18*(5), 765–783.

Grant, W. J., Moon, B., & Grant, J. B. (2010). Digital dialogue? Australian politicians' use of the social network tool Twitter. *Australian Journal of Political Science*, *45*(4), 579–604.

Grčar, M., Cherepnalkoski, D., Mozetič, I., & Novak, P. K. (2017). Stance and influence of Twitter users regarding the Brexit referendum. *Computational Social Networks*, *4*(6), 1–25. doi:10.1186/s40649-017-0042-6

Groshek, J., & Engelbert, J. (2013). Double differentiation in a cross-national comparison of populist political movements and online media uses in the United States and The Netherlands. *New Media & Society*, *15*(2), 183–202.

Gunnarsson Lorentzen, D. (2014). Polarisation in political Twitter conversations. *Aslib Journal of Information Management*, *66*(3), 329–341.

Gusterson, H. (2017). From Brexit to Trump: Anthropology and the rise of nationalist populism. *American Ethnologist, 44*(2), 209–214.

Habermas, J. (2016). For A democratic polarisation: How to pull the ground from under Right-Wing populism. *Social Europe*. Retrieved from https://www.socialeurope.eu/democratic-polarisation-pull-ground-right-wing-populism

Hallin, D. C. (1989). *The uncensored war: The media and Vietnam*. Berkeley, CA: University of California Press.

Hall, W., Tinati, R., & Jennings, W. (2018). From Brexit to Trump: Social media's role in democracy. *Computer, 51*(1), 18–27.

Harris, L., & Harrigan, P. (2015). Social media in politics: The ultimate voter engagement tool or simply an echo chamber? *Journal of Political Marketing, 14*(3), 251–283. doi:10.1080/15377857.2012.693059

Hay, C., & Smith, N. (2005). Horses for courses? The political discourse of globalisation and European integration in the UK and Ireland. *West European Politics, 28*(1), 124–158. doi:10.1080/0140238042000297116

Hebdige, D. (2016). (i) From culture to hegemony; (ii) Subculture: The unnatural break. In M. G. Durham & D. M. Kellner (Eds.), *Media and culture studies: Keyworks* (pp. 144–162). Malden, MA; Oxford; Victoria, BC: Blackwell Publishing.

Himelboim, I., Hansen, D., & Bowser, A. (2013). Playing in the same Twitter network: Political information seeking in the 2010 US gubernatorial elections. *Information, Communication & Society, 16*(9), 1373–1396.

Hobolt, S. B. (2016). The Brexit vote: A divided nation, a divided continent. *Journal of European Public Policy, 23*(9), 1259–1277.

Höijer, B. (2010). Emotional anchoring and objectification in the media reporting on climate change. *Public Understanding of Science, 19*(6), 717–731.

Höijer, B. (2011). Social representations theory: A new theory for media research. *Nordicom Review, 32*(2), 3–16.

Hong, S., & Kim, S. H. (2016). Political polarization on Twitter: Implications for the use of social media in digital governments. *Government Information Quarterly, 33*(4), 777–782.

Horan, T. J. (2013). 'Soft' versus 'hard' news on microblogging networks semantic analysis of Twitter produsage. *Information, Communication & Society*, *16*(1), 43–60.

Howard, P. N., & Kollanyi, B. (2016). Bots,# StrongerIn, and# Brexit: Computational propaganda during the UK-EU referendum. *Comprop Research Note*.

Huber, G. A., & Malhotra, N. (2017). Political homophily in social relationships: Evidence from online dating behavior. *The Journal of Politics*, *79*(1), 269–283.

Huberty, C. J. (2000). Judgement in quantitative research. *The Mathematics Educator*, *10*(1), 5–10.

Huckfeldt, R., Johnson, P. E., & Sprague, J. (2004). *Political disagreement : The survival of diverse opinions within communication networks*. New York, NY: Cambridge University Press.

Huckfeldt, R. R., & Sprague, J. (2006). *Citizens, politics and social communication: Information and influence in an election campaign*. Cambridge: Cambridge University Press.

Iakhnis, E., Rathbun, B., Reifler, J., & Scotto, T. J. (2018). Populist referendum: Was 'Brexit' an expression of nativist and anti-elitist sentiment? *Research and Politics*. doi:10.1177/2053168018773964

Ifukor, P. (2010). "Elections" or "selections"? Blogging and Twittering the Nigerian 2007 general elections. *Bulletin of Science, Technology & Society*, *30*(6), 398–414.

Inglehart, R., & Norris, P. (2016). Trump, Brexit, and the rise of populism: Economic have-nots and cultural backlash. HKS Working Paper, No. RWP16-026. doi:10.2139/ssrn.2818659

Jackson, N., & Lilleker, D. (2011). Microblogging, constituency service and impression management: UK MPs and the use of Twitter. *The Journal of Legislative Studies*, *17*(1), 86–105.

Jaidka, K., Zhou, A., & Lelkes, Y. (2020). Brevity is the soul of Twitter: The constraint affordance and political discussion. *Journal of Communication*, *69*(4), 345–372. doi:10.1093/joc/jqz023

Jamieson, K. H., & Cappella, J. (2008). *Echo chamber: Rush Limbaugh and the conservative media establishment*. London: Oxford University Press.

Kagarlitsky, B. (2017). Brexit and the future of the left. *Globalizations*, *14*(1), 110–117. doi:10.1080/14747731.2016.1228800

Kaltwasser, C. R. (2012). The ambivalence of populism: Threat and corrective for democracy. *Democratization*, *19*(2), 184–208. doi:10.1080/13510347.2011.572619

Kang, S., Ha, J.-S., & Velasco, T. (2017). Attention deficit hyperactivity disorder on YouTube: Framing, anchoring, and objectification in social media. *Community Mental Health Journal*, *53*(4), 445–451.

Karlsen, R., & Enjolras, B. (2016). Styles of social media campaigning and influence in a hybrid political communication system: Linking candidate survey data with Twitter data. *The International Journal of Press/Politics*, *21*(3), 338–357.

Keller, F. B., Schoch, D., Stier, S., & Yang, J. (2020). Political astroturfing on Twitter: How to coordinate a disinformation campaign. *Political Communication*, *37*(2), 256–280. doi:10.1080/10584609.2019.166188

Kelsey, D. (2016). Hero mythology and Right-Wing populism. *Journalism Studies*, *17*(8), 971–988. doi:10.1080/1461670X.2015.102357

Klinger, U. (2013). Mastering the art of social media: Swiss parties, the 2011 national election and digital challenges. *Information, Communication & Society*, *16*(5), 717–736.

Klofstad, C. A., Sokhey, A. E., & McClurg, S. D. (2012). Disagreeing about disagreement: How conflict in social networks affects political behavior. *American Journal of Political Science*, *57*(1), 120–134.

Klonick, K. (2019). Inside the team at Facebook that dealt with the Christchurch shooting. *The New Yorker*. Retrieved from https://www.newyorker.com/news/news-desk/inside-the-team-at-facebook-that-dealt-with-the-christchurch-shooting

Krämer, B. (2017). Populist online practices: The function of the Internet in Right-Wing populism. *Information, Communication & Society*, *20*(9), 1293–1309. doi:10.1080/1369118X.2017.13285

Kreis, R. (2017). The "tweet politics" of President Trump. *Journal of Language and Politics*, *16*(4), 607–618.

Lachlan, K. A., & Levy, D. R. (2016). BIRGing, CORFing, and Twitter activity following a political referendum: Examining social media activity concerning the 2014 Scottish independence vote. *Communication Research Reports*, *33*(3), 217–222.

Larsson, A. O., & Ihlen, Ø. (2015). Birds of a feather flock together? Party leaders on Twitter during the 2013 Norwegian elections. *European Journal of Communication*, *30*(6), 666–681.

Larsson, A. O., & Moe, H. (2014). Triumph of the underdogs? Comparing Twitter use by political actors during two Norwegian election campaigns. *Sage Open*, *4*(4).

Lasorsa, D. (2012). Transparency and other journalistic norms on Twitter. *Journalism Studies*, *13*(3), 402–417.

Lawless, B., & Chen, Y.-W. (2019). Developing a method of critical thematic analysis for qualitative communication inquiry. *Howard Journal of Communications*, *30*(1), 92–106. doi:10.1080/10646175.2018.1439423

Lewis, S. C., Zamith, R., & Hermida, A. (2013). Content analysis in an era of big data: A hybrid approach to computational and manual methods. *Journal of Broadcasting & Electronic Media*, *57*(1), 34–52.

Lindgren, S., & Cocq, C. (2017). Turning the inside out: Social media and the broadcasting of indigenous discourse. *European Journal of Communication*, *32*(2), 131–150.

Linvill, D. L., & Warren, P. L. (2020). Troll factories: Manufacturing specialized disinformation on Twitter. *Political Communication*. doi:10.1080/10584609.2020.1718257

Lischka, J. A. (2019). A badge of honor?. *Journalism Studies*, *20*(2), 287–304. doi:10.1080/1461670X.2017.1375385

Llewellyn, C., & Cram, L. (2016). Brexit? Analyzing opinion on the UK-EU referendum within Twitter. Paper presented at the Tenth International AAAI Conference on Web and Social Media.

Lopez, A. D., Cesar, J., Collignon-Delma, S., Benoit, K., & Matsuo, A. (2017). Predicting the Brexit vote by tracking and classifying public opinion using Twitter data. *Statistics, Politics and Policy*, *8*(1), 85–104.

Loughborough University. (2016). Media coverage of the EU Referendum (report 5).

Lugg, A. N. (2013). Mantous and alpacas as weapons of the weak: Chinese spoof video and self-expression online. *First Monday*, *18*(7). doi:10.5210/fm.v18i7.3885

Lynch, P. (2010). Cameron, modernisation and conservative Britain. In S. Griffith & K. Hickson (Eds.), *British party politics and ideology after new labour* (pp. 119–134). London: Palgrave Macmillan.

Manovich, L. (2009). The practice of everyday (media) life: From mass consumption to mass cultural production? *Critical Inquiry*, *35*(2), 319–331.

Margolin, D. B., Hannak, A., & Weber, I. (2018). Political fact-checking on Twitter: When do corrections have an effect? *Political Communication*, *35*(2), 196–219. doi:10.1080/10584609.2017.1334018

Mazzoleni, G. (2008). Populism and the media. In D. Albertazzi & D. McDonnell (Eds.), *Twenty-first century populism* (pp. 49–64). London: Palgrave Macmillan.

McCombs, M. E., & Shaw, D. L. (1972). The agenda setting function of the mass media. *Public Opinion Quarterly*, *36*(2), 176–187.

McNair, B. (2004). PR must die: Spin, anti-spin and political public relations in the UK, 1997–2004. *Journalism Studies*, *5*(3), 325–338.

McPherson, J. M., & Smith-Lovin, L. (1987). Homophily in voluntary organizations: Status distance and the composition of face-to-face groups. *American Sociological Review*, *52*(3), 370–379.

McPherson, M., Smith-Lovin, L., & Cook, J. M. (2001). Birds of a feather: Homophily in social networks. *Annual Review of Sociology*, *27*(1), 415–444.

Meraz, S. (2009). Is there an elite hold? Traditional media to social media agenda setting influence in blog networks. *Journal of Computer-Mediated Communication*, *14*(3), 682–707.

Meraz, S., & Papacharissi, Z. (2013). Networked gatekeeping and networked framing on# Egypt. *The International Journal of Press/Politics*, *18*(2), 138–166.

Messing, S., & Westwood, S. J. (2014). Selective exposure in the age of social media: Endorsements Trump partisan source affiliation when selecting news online. *Communication Research*, *41*(8), 1042–1063.

Milner, H. V. (2019). Globalisation, populism and the decline of the welfare state. *Survival: Global Politics and Strategy*, *61*(2), 91–96. doi:10.1080/00396338.2019.1589087

Mondon, A. (2013). *The Mainstreaming of the extreme right in France and Australia: A populist Hegemony?* Oxon; New York, NY: Routledge.

Moscovici, S. (2001). *Social representations: Explorations in social psychology*. Cambridge: New York University Press.

Moscovici, S., & Markova, I. (1998). Presenting social representations: A conversation. *Culture & Psychology*, *4*(3), 371–410.

Mounk, Y. (2014). Pitchfork politics: The populist threat to liberal democracy. *Foreign Affairs*, *93*(27), 27–36.

Mutz, D. C. (2006). *Hearing the other side: Deliberative versus participatory democracy*. New York, NY: Cambridge University Press.

Öztürk, N., & Ayvaz, S. (2018). Sentiment analysis on Twitter: A text mining approach to the Syrian refugee crisis. *Telematics and Informatics*, *35*(1), 136–147.

Painter, A. (2013). Democratic stress, the populist signal and extremist threat. *Policy network*, *56*.

Papacharissi, Z., & Easton, E. (2013). In the habitus of the new. In J. Hartley, J. Burgess, & A. Bruns (Eds.), *A companion to new media dynamics* (*Vols. 171–184*). Oxford: Wiley-Blackwell.

Pariser, E. (2011). *The filter bubble: What the internet is hiding from you*. London: Viking.

Park, C. S. (2013). Does Twitter motivate involvement in politics? Tweeting, opinion leadership, and political engagement. *Computers in Human Behavior*, *29*(4), 1641–1648.

Payne, R. (2018). Brexit and the British media. *The Round Table: The Commonwealth Journal of International Affairs*, *107*(1), 109–110. doi: 10.1080/00358533.2018.1424083

Peters, M. A. (2018). The end of neoliberal globalisation and the rise of authoritarian populism. *Educational Philosophy and Theory*, *50*(4), 323–325. doi:10.1080/00131857.2017.1305720

Pilipets, E., & Winter, R. (2017). Repeat, remediate, resist? Digital meme activism in the context of the refugee crisis. In J. Wimmer, C. Wallner, R. Winter, & K. Oelsner (Eds.), *(Mis) Understanding political participation: Digital practices, new forms of participation and the renewal of democracy*. London; New York, NY: Routledge.

Pond, P., & Lewis, J. (2019). Riots and Twitter: Connective politics, social media and framing discourses in the digital public sphere. *Information, Communication & Society*, *22*(2), 213–231.

Postill, J. (2018). Populism and social media: A global perspective. *Media, Culture & Society*, *40*(5), 754–765.

Rauchfleisch, A., & Metag, J. (2016). The special case of Switzerland: Swiss politicians on Twitter. *New Media & Society*, *18*(10), 2413–2431. doi: 10.1177/1461444815586982

Rehurek, R., & Sojka, P. (2010). Software framework for topic modelling with large corpora. Paper presented at the Proceedings of the LREC 2010 workshop on new challenges for NLP frameworks, Valletta, Malta. Retrieved from https://radimrehurek.com/gensim/lrec2010_final.pdf

Reinemann, C., Aalberg, T., Esser, F., Strömbäck, J., & de Vreese, C. H. (2017). Populist political communication: Toward a model of its causes, forms, and effects. In T. Aalberg, F. Esser, C. Reinemann, J. Strömbäck, & C. H. de Vreese (Eds.), *Populist political communication in Europe* (pp. 12–25). New York, NY: Routledge.

Rooduijn, M. (2014). The mesmerising message: The diffusion of populism in public debates in Western European media. *Political Studies*, *62*(4), 726–744.

Sargent, L. T. (2009). *Contemporary political ideologies: A comparative analysis*. Belmont, CA: WADSWORTH Cengage Learning.

Sayre, B., Bode, L., Shah, D., Wilcox, D., & Shah, C. (2010). Agenda setting in a digital age: Tracking attention to California proposition 8 in social media, online news, and conventional news. Article 2. *Policy & Internet*, *2*(2). doi: 10.2202/1944-2866.1040

Schreiber, M. (2017). Audiences, aesthetics and affordances analysing practices of visual communication on social media. *Digital Culture & Society*, *3*(2), 143–164.

Schulz, A., & Roessler, P. (2012). The spiral of silence and the Internet: Selection of online content and the perception of public opinion climate in computer-mediated communication environments. *International Journal of Public Opinion Research*, *24*(3), 346–367.

Sears, D. O., & Freedman, J. L. (1967). Selective exposure to information: A critical review. *Public Opinion Quarterly*, *31*(2), 194–213.

Seaton, J. (2016). Brexit and the media. *The Political Quarterly*, *87*(3), 333–337.

Smithson, A.-B., & Vraga, E. K. (2017). I beg to differ. In J. C. Baumgartner & T. L. Towner (Eds.), *The internet and the 2016 presidential campaign* (pp. 51–77). Lanham, MD: Lexington Books.

Sobkowicz, P., Kaschesky, M., & Bouchard, G. (2012). Opinion mining in social media: Modeling, simulating, and forecasting political opinions in the web. *Government Information Quarterly*, *29*(4), 470–479.

Spiering, M. (2004). British Euroscepticism. In R. Harmsen & M. Spiering (Eds.), *Euroscepticism: Party politics, national identity and European integration* (pp. 127–149). Amersterdam; New York, NY: Rodopi.

Startin, N. (2015). Have we reached a tipping point? The mainstreaming of Euroscepticism in the UK. *International Political Science Review*, *36*(3), 311–323.

Stier, S., Posch, L., Bleier, A., & Strohmaier, M. (2017). When populists become popular: Comparing Facebook use by the Right-Wing movement Pegida and German political parties. *Information, Communication & Society*, *20*(9), 1365–1388.

Sunstein, C. R. (2009). *Republic.com 2.0*. New York, NY: Princeton UP.

Sunstein, C. R. (2018). *# Republic: Divided democracy in the age of social media*. Princeton, NJ; Oxford: Princeton University Press.

Taggart, P. (2004). Populism and representative politics in contemporary Europe. *Journal of Political Ideologies*, *9*(3). doi:10.1080/1356931042000263528

Tantawi, Y., & Rosson, M. B. (2019). The paralinguistic function of emojis in Twitter communication. Social Media Corpora for the Humanities (p. 68).

The BBC. (2016, April 13th, 2016). Lead EU referendum campaigns named. *The BBC*. Retrieved from https://www.bbc.co.uk/news/uk-politics-36038672

The Economist. (2020, June 4th, 2020). A tale of two social networks: Twitter and Facebook have differing business models. *The Economist*. Retrieved from https://www.economist.com/business/2020/06/04/twitter-and-facebook-have-differing-business-models

Tong, J., & Zuo, L. (2017). Practising journalism on Twitter? A computational analysis of British journalists' use of Twitter before the 2016 EU referendum in the UK. In J. Tong & S.-h. Lo (Eds.), *Technology and journalism: From an international comparative perspective*. London: Palgrave.

Tong, J., & Zuo, L. (2018). *Tweeting the environment #Brexit*. Bingley: Emerald Publishing Limited.

Tong, J., & Zuo, L. (2019). Othering the European Union through constructing moral panics over 'im/migrant(s)' in the coverage of migration in three British newspapers, 2011–2016. *International Communication Gazette*, *81*(5), 445–469. doi:10.1177/1748048518802237

Trottier, D. (2012). Interpersonal surveillance on social media. *Canadian Journal of Communication*, *37*(2), 319–332.

Tully, M., & Ekdale, B. (2014). Sites of playful engagement: Twitter hashtags as spaces of leisure and development in Kenya. *Information Technologies and International Development*, *10*(3), 67–82.

Uphama, P., Lis, A., Rieschc, H., & Stankiewiczd, P. (2015). Addressing social representations in socio-technical transitions with the case of shale gas. *Environmental Innovation and Societal Transitions*, *16*, 120–141.

Usherwood, S., & Wright, K. A. (2017). Sticks and stones: Comparing Twitter campaigning strategies in the European Union referendum. *The British Journal of Politics & International Relations*, *19*(2), 371–388.

Vaccari, C., Valeriani, A., Barberá, P., Jost, J. T., Nagler, J., & Tucker, J. A. (2016). Of echo chambers and contrarian clubs: Exposure to political disagreement among German and Italian users of Twitter. *Social Media + Society*. Retrieved from https://journals.sagepub.com/doi/pdf/10.1177/2056305116664221

Valenzuela, S., Correa, T., & Zúñiga, H. G. d. (2018). Ties, likes, and tweets: Using strong and weak ties to explain differences in protest participation across Facebook and Twitter use. *Political Communication*, *35*(1), 117–134.

Vasilopoulou, S. (2016). UK Euroscepticism and the Brexit referendum. *The Political Quarterly*, *87*(2), 219–227.

Veltri, G. A. (2013). Microblogging and nanotweets: Nanotechnology on Twitter. *Public Understanding of Science*, *22*(7), 832–849.

Veltri, G. A., & Atanasova, D. (2017). Climate change on Twitter: Content, media ecology and information sharing behaviour. *Public Understanding of Science*, *26*(6), 721–737.

Von Bogdandy, A., & Nettesheim, M. (1996). Ex pluribus unum: Fusion of the European Communities into the European Union. *European Law Journal*, *2*(3), 267–289.

Vreese, C. H. d., Esser, F., Aalberg, T., Reinemann, C., & Stanyer, J. (2018). Populism as an expression of political communication content and style: A new perspective. *The International Journal of Press/Politics*, *23*(4), 423–438.

Waisbord, S. (2003). Media populism: Neo-populism in Latin America. In G. Mazzoleni, J. Stewart, & B. Horsfield (Eds.), *The media and neo-populism: A contemporary comparative analysis* (pp. 197–217). Westport: Praeger Publishers.

Weyland, K. (2013). Latin America's authoritarian drift: The threat from the populist left. *Journal of Democracy*, *24*(3), 18–32.

Williams, R. (2016). Base and superstructure in Marxist cultural theory. In M. G. Durham, & D. M. Kellner (Eds.), *Media and culture studies: Keyworks* (pp. 130–143). Malden, MA; Oxford; Victoria, BC: Blackwell Publishing.

Wodak, R. (2009). *The discourse of politics in action*. London: Palgrave Macmillan.

Wright, S., Graham, T., & Jackson, D. (2016). Third space, social media and everyday political talk. In A. Bruns, G. Enli, E. Skogerbo, A. O. Larsson, & C. Christensen (Eds.), *The Routledge companion to social media and politics* (pp. 74–88). New York, NY: Routledge.

Yang, J. H., Barnidge, M., & Rojas, H. (2017). The politics of"Unfriending": User filtration in response to political disagreement on social media. *Computers in Human Behavior*, *70*, 22–29.

Yılmaz, F. (2006). Ethnicized ontologies: From foreign worker to muslim immigrant: How Danish public discourse moved to the right through the question of immigration. PhD, UC San Diego. Retrieved from https://escholarship.org/content/qt8fd0g7h7/qt8fd0g7h7.pdf

Zappavigna, M. (2015). Searchable talk: The linguistic functions of hashtags. *Social Semiotics*, *25*(3). doi:10.1080/10350330.10352014.10399694

Zappavigna, M., & Zhao, S. (2020). Selfies and recontextualization: Still life self-imaging in social media. In M. Miles & E. Welch (Eds.), *Photography and its publics*. London: Bloomsbury.

Zhu, Q., Skoric, M., & Shen, F. (2017). I shield myself from thee: Selective avoidance on social media during political protests. *Political Communication*, *34*(1), 112–131. doi:10.1080/10584609.2016.1222471

Zulianello, M., Albertini, A., & Ceccobelli, D. (2018). A populist Zeitgeist? The communication strategies of Western and Latin American political leaders on Facebook. *The International Journal of Press/Politics*, *23*(4), 439–457.

INDEX